The King's Book

Manager Skills

Marketing

Brand

Sales

Thank you to my beloved wife, Veronika!

The champions are moving on!

Striving from the bottom up is inexhaustible. No matter what grounds philosophers and psychologists think about - self-preservation, principles of pleasure, equalization - all this is nothing more than remote representations of the great movement upwards!

Alfred Adler

The main task of a person's life is to give life to himself, to become what he is potential. The most important fruit of his efforts is his personality

Erich Fro

Table of Contents

Chapter 1 Significance.

Hello, this is my first book on marketing, sales, and branding. As of the end of 2019, I have experience working in two international companies in the field of Fast Moving Consumer Goods, the most top sellers of their products in many countries around the world. I formed sales teams many years ago, my eyes were burning with new challenges, and I wanted to prove myself. So I grew from a supervisor to a national-level marketing manager. I had 55 cities under my command and about 300 people in direct management. I have never been embarrassed by the scale and vast geography. On the contrary, these challenges corresponded to my ambitions. I want more and do more than I am expected to do. And I like it. I do it with my soul, with thoughts about you, my reader. I want to give you the grain of truth and experience that I was able to carry within me. In some ways, I won't be able to call it all my names. Where I am, it's the inner family of every company, but I can talk about the good and positive things that have become a springboard for me!

1. What's the Background to Me?

We are advertising, sales, media, pr, etc. Managers are people with a creative and mathematical composition of mind. Which always requires continuous work and moving towards the goal. I always say to myself, "when I stand, I fall. I want to say that development is to develop it during the period of quality and quality, at different rates, sometimes practically slowing down, but never stopping. My dear reader, I am sure that you need quantitative indicators of my experience, here they are.

After working for more than 3 years in big companies, I felt the power to create my own, something creative and capacious.

On May 25, 2011, I became a co-founder and managing partner of a marketing company and became a co-founder with high hopes and ambitions. I already had a successful experience in managing and coordinating hundreds of people and started to understand the basic financial flows of the advertising market, PR, Marketing and Media.

My competencies:

-Formation of the sales department

-Formation of the project implementation department

-Direct negotiations with clients

-Human Resource

-Public Relation

Having set myself great goals, I began to perform great tasks. I created my Z sheet for myself. I identified the brands that had good marketing budgets, chose those that I liked better, and started to work on. At first, I collected information from open sources. Later, I studied what vacancies they had open and what tenders had been held earlier.

This list included marketing departments of various brands, advertising, and sales of top campaigns.

Johnie Walker, Jose Cuervo, Captain Morgan, Baileys, Coca-Cola, Imperial Tabaco, GTI, Haggis, Adidas, Syngenta, Shabo, and many others that I will cover in this book.

During this time, together with the team, we were able to implement and participate in more than 1000 projects in 10 years. In May 2013, the marketing campaign was conducted simultaneously with more than 30 projects involving more than 700 people. During the three years of management, the team and I managed to achieve good results, and the campaign case study began to show serious clients and serious projects.

Working with tops taught us speed, flexibility, and creativity. These three words are the main pillars in the formation and support of relationships with brands. And of course, you have to be a professional.

Direct sales, sales department formation, marketing, advertising, public relations gave me new opportunities, which I certainly used.

This book, a book from the heart. It is an experience carved from stone. It is a competence that will always be at the heart of my internal manager. There are no unfulfilled tasks. There are wrong instructions!

I will talk about the philosophy of global market campaigns. About brand building, finding new customers, and the role of marketing for the latest breakthrough, the team, and the sales department as a whole! To upgrade already that knowledge that you have been able to get yourself experience on the education of your life. This is not a step-by-step instruction for beginners. It is a facet of a diamond, a field in which millions of people work. It's a field of inspiration, a third look from the outside. Of course, with your insides. With this book, I want to pave the way for hundreds of miles between us. This is an era of opportunity; let's use it together!

P.S. Dear reader, I need your support! I will continue to carry the torch for other people!

2. The Brand Age.

Today, a person faces a lot of similar brands, which have saturated with the market. To understand them, a person does not have enough time physically. In this situation, the brand dramatically simplifies the process of choosing what to label each product: "Expensive but prestigious", "Economical and practical.

Brand - is an intangible sum of the properties of the product, namely - its name, history, reputation, packaging, price, and method of advertising.

I determine the success of the brand by the following characteristics: the number of advertising costs, uniqueness of the product, quality of packaging design, the presence of a significant conceptual idea and the degree of its compliance with the wishes of the consumer and, of course, the properties of the product itself.

The relevance of the work, markets are growing and the era of brands. Market development is accompanied by active growth and aggravation of competition between participants.

The lifestyle is changing, security and comfort requirements among the population are growing. What did the consumer want 20 years ago? The main requirements were durability and longevity, but now the brand, beauty, comfort and other values that a brand can give are in the foreground when choosing a product. This shows the growth of consumer culture. Children's clothes, toys, books require constant updating, and this ensures the market turnover.

Stories from the manager's life

Adidas AG

How to succeed. When I opened my Excel spreadsheet, there were different giants in the advertising market. One of them was the Adidas brand and its advertising department. I can say that they are real professionals, open to suggestions, but carefully choose whom to work with. We had a series of meetings, we had phone calls beforehand, we sent all our presentations, and we applied for the tender. A year and a half passed from the moment of the first contact to the project implementation. Quick results are temporary, the best things to build, implement and create.

3. If the Brand Loves to Forgive Him a Lot.

Consumers prefer a brand when brand messages are objective, and their values are positioned. The main task of a brand is to identify, express these features and inform consumers about its advantages. Studying the consumer's perception of the quality of the product gives you the opportunity to get the information necessary for the development of the brand project and the positioning of its values. In order to increase brand value in the eyes of consumers, the following procedures should be implemented.

Manufacturers also prefer to receive objective information about brand values, as this is the only basis on which a friendly attitude to the brand is formed, which, in turn, contributes to the sale of goods at higher prices, makes it possible to expand the position of the brand and stimulate the effectiveness of marketing technology.

The ability of a brand to fulfil its mission is the main characteristic of its quality.

Each product group has its specific quality criteria. Product quality is an essential factor that shapes consumer attitudes towards the brand. It should be noted that qualitative characteristics offered by the manufacturer and qualitative characteristics expected by the consumer may not only not coincide, but even differ significantly from each other.

Consumers perceive the quality of products not as a level of progressive technology of product manufacturing, but as a product reflecting the quality consumer properties of goods.

Consumer quality of the brand is determined by the choice, search, purchase, use, and whether the expectations in the purchase of this product were met.

Studying the consumer's perception of the quality of the product provides an opportunity to obtain the information necessary for the development of the brand project and the positioning of its values.

A well-known brand always enjoys a certain sympathy and respect. However, compassion and respect for the brand must be maintained. To maintain this position, it is necessary to consistently and timely update the proposals on brand values, new shades of product quality and all its other characteristics. Such an update allows the brand to make products the basis of their communications and form a favourable image.

4. How to Evaluate the Brand Image?

Image - a set of ideas, developed in the public opinion about how a person should behave, in accordance with their status!

Image is created by PR, propaganda, advertising, lies in order to create in the mass consciousness a certain attitude to this object. It can combine real properties of an object as well as non-existent, attributed, and fictitious ones.

Image study is engaged in image science. The process of image creation is called imaging.

Image should be measured

- How the client, the consumer perceives

- Consumer satisfaction

- Unique name, originality

- Brand and portrait of the consumer, compliance.

- Social work, promises, and delivery

- Distinctive characteristics in terms of product quality

5. Image Building.

A brand manager should strive for effective communication with consumers, through which they can create a qualitative impression. Today, neither product nor technology can be the primary means of promoting the brand because the consumer is at the heart of all business decisions. Therefore, the brand should develop the individuality of the consumer and which brings him pleasure from the self-awareness of its importance, to create its image.

A consumer's imaginary image should be in harmony with his life goals. To do this, it is necessary to identify and select useful emotional characteristics of the brand, which will motivate and exceed the needs of consumers in self-image - the feeling of a person's individuality.

The essence of brand loyalty is determined by a subjective factor of expanding borders, within which the change of the brand does not lead to qualitative changes in the consumer's behaviour. If these characteristics, such as quality, assortment, price, in the buyer's view, go beyond what is allowed, then the consumer uses other brands.

Consumer behaviour is affected by many factors: price increases; declining quality of goods; unstable quality; insufficient assortment; prolonged absence of goods from the point of sale; temporary absence from the point of sale; poor quality of warranty and service; and failure to keep the promises made by the manufacturer.

Buyer behaviour also depends on the ability to forgive minor errors and roughness associated with production technology.

With the systematic strengthening of customer-brand relations, the degree of loyalty increases.

As the market situation changes and competition intensifies, brand loyalty allows the firm to retain the majority of its customers.

The main task of the relationship management mechanism is to form long-term, mutually beneficial brand relations with consumers based on a strong emotional connection. This approach creates conscious loyalty to the brand.

Consider the fundamental relationships with brand and brand customers

Ability to communicate with a customer. The relationship between the brand and the consumer depends on how well the partners conduct the dialogue. If manufacturers do not have regular discussions with customers, they will not know anything about their needs and interests. Consumers of the brand, in turn, will feel disinterested in their needs. If the brand consistently maintains good relations with actual customers, continually meets their expectations, they become the best customers and potential customers of the brand.

Brand orientation to the consumer is the key to the success of the relationship management mechanism.

The traditional model of customer relationship management has quite a logical basis - product orientation. This approach is typical even for new high-tech industries, where technology is the main focus. The internal potential of a company is determined when modelling a product-oriented brand.

The most effective approach to customer relationship management is customer orientation. This approach should seek to create a strong brand through the buyer. It is necessary to study its potential and real customers.

The formation of the process of management of mutual relations, it is necessary to be guided by the following principles:

-studying the interests and needs of the buyer;

–a comprehensive study of customers based on information about contacts and channels of communication with them.

Communication between the brand and the consumer is carried out by various means; by phone, mail, through the Internet, thanks to personal contact. Communication channels must be open to the customer so that he or she can communicate with the brand without difficulty.

Consumer information support. The customer needs to be informed about: brand potential, brand development strategies, and negative factors affecting brand development.

Information support of the customer relationship management process should be clear, and objective: how often they buy, how much they buy, how much they buy last, what they do not accept in the brand, what competing brands buy, why they do not buy the brand.

Creating a comprehensive program of information support for the customer relationship management process involves creating a database that combines all the main characteristics of the functioning and development of the brand.

These principles contribute to the development of tactics of customer relationship management, and in the end - the formation of a close relationship between the brand and the customer based on knowledge about it. This approach blocks the actions of competitors, a good understanding of the consumer - beyond the competition.

To develop proposals for the development of brand values, the following procedures should be implemented.

Analysis of all subsystems of the company. It is necessary to analyze all links connected with the collection, processing, and storage of information about customers. Sales, marketing and accounting subsystems, application and proposal processing subsystems, after-sales service, credit control subsystems are subject to analysis.

The analysis of the information on buyers, gathering, and storage. The analysis of the information on buyers is carried out in the following directions:

in what form each information element is presented - in the form of text, number, per cent;

how the data collection process is organized;

Efficiency, timeliness of information receipt, its age, and reliability.

Analysis of the relationship system. When analyzing the system of brand relations with consumers, it is necessary to identify the extent to which customers contribute to its dissemination. The ability of a brand to expand, to increase demand, is called elasticity. Brand elasticity depends on purposeful attention to the customer and is formed based on a unified approach to the selection of target customers with certain characteristics and taking into account specific situations.

Analysis of the financial subsystem. The financial analysis allows us to determine how effective the process of customer relationship management is. Therefore at the formation of the mechanism of management of mutual relations with buyers, it is necessary to carry out its technical and economic substantiation.

Development of the strategy of development of the process of customer relationship management. It should be carried out in interrelation with the brand strategy based on the analysis and feasibility study of effective customer relationship management. In most cases, buyers are aware of more than one brand in this category. Therefore, their choice will be based on brand attitude. On average, 35-40% of brands that the consumer is aware of are considered acceptable by them, but usually, they have to choose one of them.

Attitudes towards the brand are the most complex of the effects of communication. Brand attitude includes four main components:

- persuasion - attitude

- benefit-sharing

- possible autonomous emotions

Belief is the mental link between the brand and the customer's motivation. Belief is the attitude. The customer's attitude towards the brand in the brain connects the brand to the drive to buy.

One of the essential components of a brand attitude is one or more opinions about the specific benefits the brand provides.

These views on specific benefits are due to the rational content of marketing communication.

The creation of a relationship is an objective when the audience has not yet had an impression of the brand when the customer does not know anything about it.

Chapter 2 Why Does Marketing Work for Some and Not for Others?

"Marketing is a waste of time and money if you are going to offer your customers a low-quality product or service. Because in this case, the better your marketing is, the more people will know that you are selling trash, the faster it will happen - and the faster your firm will go bankrupt."

Jay Conrad Levinson, the founding father of guerrilla marketing

You are marketing. If they don't know you, how can you teach someone to recognize you?

One day, my friends invited me to take a walk around town in the evening. We haven't seen each other for a long time. We were about 10 people. Guys and girls are all from the sphere of marketing, sales, and branding. My friends didn't know that I had opened a marketing company at the time and was actively looking for new customers. Among my friends were strangers, one of them a guy from Turkey. He saw a funny Bord ad board, and we started talking about it. During the conversation, he said that I was the owner of a marketing campaign. Among the new acquaintances was the marketing director of a large network of gadgets and accessories. Their presence in 20 cities, the network has 60 specialized stores. In a friendly atmosphere, we agreed to start cooperation, and in 3 months we serviced the stores in all representative offices. What conclusion did I make?

Expand your environment correctly and make sure that in the era of branding and influential people, your marketing works too.

Why is this happening?

A typical situation in which entrepreneurs find themselves.

No clients - no sales, no sales - no business, no system for attracting clients - no clients. The circle is closed.

There are a number of reasons and factors. I will highlight 5 key sources of failure:

- Low-quality products and services

- Lack of a clear system for attracting and retaining clients.

- Lack of understanding of the target audience, its needs, and motives

- Lack of positioning and differentiation from competitors

- Lack of control over the efficiency of marketing budget use.

What is the attitude of most entrepreneurs towards marketing? "Dinosaurs" and "Transformers

Let's see how most entrepreneurs feel about marketing.

The category "Dinosaurs" refers to people who do not believe in marketing at all. They don't believe and don't understand why they need it.

Such business people are sure that they will achieve everything by themselves and without marketing. They believe in the genius of their idea. Often it is these beliefs that prevent them from rebuilding themselves and their business. Why do these entrepreneurs not believe in marketing?

They don't understand what a marketing manager in their company should do:

-Attracting clients?

-Customer retention?

-Why, if it is possible to "hang" on sales managers.

-Why, if the old ones leave, we will find new ones.

When such an approach leads a company to a crisis, when sales volume and profits start to dive sharply, these entrepreneurs start looking for all possible ways to keep their business afloat. They are moving into the second category.

Transformers' entrepreneurs already understand that marketing is vital for their organizations.

It should be an integral and irreplaceable part of a living organism. But there is one striking fact: as soon as business people from this category start to engage in marketing, they expect magic from him. Every penny invested in marketing should immediately bring millions, and customers should crowd at the front door of the office.Entrepreneurs in this group see marketing as magic.

Marketing, in their opinion, should also immediately solve all the existing problems of the organization. Entrepreneurs are beginning to grab any tools they want: they implement pieces of one tool, then another. Having lost money, they are disappointed in marketing and return to the first category - entrepreneurs who believe they can do without marketing.

Why is this happening?

The answer is one - marketing should be systematic and planned. It can be compared to sports activities. If a person is overweight, and he once went to the gym, once jogged and swam in the pool, and waits for the effect - he will not be. Daily complex sports activities remove the excess weight.

It is also necessary to treat marketing in the same way.

Chapter 3 Universal Laws of Development of The Brand. Top Marketing.

In order not to join the ranks of Dinosaurs I have written about above, you should know and remember 10 universal marketing laws for the development of your brand

Not to sell, but to satisfy the needs.

Marketing should be useful! If you don't do marketing, sooner or later, competitors will eat you.

It's just a matter of time! Because they not only do marketing, they think about how to improve it, how to be more profitable and faster. They want to surprise with their advantages, and they are continually working on it.

Loyalty is not easy: people have no reason to believe in the mission of a chocolate manufacturer, sports shoe seller, or search engine. But people can be persuaded. The only thing you need to do is to be sincerely caring, to solve people's existing problems.

Large companies often create special applications and services. They are not aimed at sales or at working with products or services of the company. Their task is to form loyalty.

This approach is used, for example, by Nike + Run Club. It helps to organize training, set goals, and monitor their achievement. It does not sell anything, and people use it all the time.

Another example from the sports industry is the Adidas All Day fitness application. It combines the functions of other sports applications and takes into account training, nutrition, and recreation for a healthy lifestyle. It guides and motivates, and its goal is to help women improve their health.

One example is Google. The company implements many special projects in the field of useful marketing.

1. Planned Marketing.

Marketing needs to be done regularly; otherwise, you will never be able to ensure the uninterrupted flow of new customers.

Content marketing and expert positioning.

Why can content marketing increase sales in your company?

Trust is one of the essential criteria when buying. Pump up trust in your company with content marketing

What is content marketing?

We use the definition of content marketing and inbound-marketing as synonyms.

My goal is to give basic insights into content marketing to owners and top managers, marketing directors, and those who want to improve their understanding of marketing.

Professionals can find new tools and mechanisms here - further recommendations from the practical knowledge gained on hundreds of client projects.

Content marketing is a way to form a stream of target requests from potential clients for your business by placing expert articles and other information on the site for their subsequent distribution in the network.

2. "My business is special and different from all others!" - Do you believe this?

Do you think you have a "unique" business and a "non-standard" situation compared to all the others? Then the following list is especially for you:

Many entrepreneurs are mistaken in the total uniqueness of their business and market

- Content marketing works efficiently and increases sales both in the B2C segment (your clients) and in the B2B segment (your corporate clients).

3. "Where is the evidence that content marketing works?

The main objective of content marketing is to establish communication and customer behaviour. Let's consider the stages that a potential customer goes through before buying, as well as the parameters on the basis of which there is a conscious or unconscious final choice between buying and not buying.

Content-marketing will form a stream of target references to the company. Should I remind you that this is money?

Most businesses work with potential clients according to the following principle: "came to the site → sent a request or made a call → bought".

What's wrong here? This is exactly what we need!

That's right; there's only one catch - at best 2-3% of the total number of visitors to the site. Yes, you can and should improve and develop your website, online store, sales platform to increase conversion.

As an average conversion is considered a good conversion of 2-3%! But what happens to other potential customers who have visited your site?

With those who did not call or did not send a request right now? Alas, in the vast majority of cases: gone and forgotten. And when we remembered, we found your competitor.

4. Stages of making a purchase decision.

Let's think about who this 2-3% of buyers are, who send an application, or place an order at once. As a rule, these are people who have already "ripened" to buy in a certain way. What stages do they go through before "maturation"? Buyer's thoughts...

- It's an interesting product. I just happened to stop by. Interesting service-goods, one day I will learn more.

- I will remember I will be useful. It is necessary to note, probably, it will be useful to me.

- Perhaps I will buy it if... "Wait for a good price, time to choose a product -service.

- Buy! "Who do I remember from the sellers of this product/service, who can recommend? - At this stage, the buyer can get to this stage, consistently passing the previous stages, or immediately, if there is an urgent need (for example, tomorrow is the birthday of his wife or husband, and the gift is not purchased in advance).

- Analysis of the place of purchase. I will choose this shop/company. I trust them, closer to home - more about the choice matrix below.

- Interest in the company, the brand. I will learn more about the product and services. It ends with the final decision about the place of purchase.

- Buying which brought joy "Pleasure from the decision").

- Confirmation of the correctness of choice... I'm good that I chose this product/service because - this is a direct way to re-purchase if its accuracy will be confirmed to myself.

The more valuable the product/service is, the more time the buyer spends to choose and buy.

So, only those who are at the stage of "Interest about the company, brand" buy from us and in the process of choosing the place of purchase found your company's website or chose your product among other brands. And what about the additional 98-97% of visitors to the site? They are all at other stages before the "Interest about the company, brand" stage. Depending on the complexity and cost of the product - all stages can be prolonged in time.

For example, when buying chocolate, all the stages are within 1 minute. When ordering a sophisticated service, a vacation tour, accounting services, website promotion, or purchasing expensive goods - the passage of the potential client stages can last for months and some - years.

Please go through all the stages of making a purchase decision with your potential customers, help them overcome the obstacles and objections!

Hence, the more complex and expensive your product service is, the longer the potential customer needs to "go through the stages." Thus, the task of content marketing is as follows: to lead the prospective client through all the stages to the stage of "Purchase that brought joy." Make sure that he remembers you at the time of purchase.

"Contact Point" is the moment when a person has received information about your company in any form, for example: entered your website, talked to the manager, received a letter from you, saw your targeted advertising. Several "points of contact" form "chain links."

What is "Point of contact"?

In marketing, there is such a concept, point of contact. It means all the ways, opportunities, and variations ways of communications between customers and potential customers and your company. As a marketing manager, you need to know all the existing and potential points of contact. Create a list of them and then do your best to make them all pleasant, fast and professional.

This is very important. During such contacts, the potential client decides whether he will work with you or not. It's a moment of truth. But it doesn't end there. For your established client, the value of the points of contact does not diminish either.

Companies always have the opportunity to compare, and if your competitors have a better relationship with customers, then, all other things being equal, he can give preference to them. Your points of contact can be very diverse.

The easiest way to figure them out is to imagine a potential customer's path to your company and an algorithm for their future interaction with you:

- Your business cards

- Your brochure

- Your company's website

- The sign outside your office

- The design of your office

- Toilet rooms

- Your meeting rooms

- Presentations made by sales managers

- The look and feel of your sales managers

- How does your secretary respond to incoming calls

- Did you offer drinks

- Have they made sure that the client has something to do if they have to wait (it is better if this does not happen, but some things happen)

- How quickly the call is forwarded to the employee the client wants to talk to.

The list can be endless. To keep your hands free, make your first list of only 10 positions. Mark the 10 most important points of contact. Now start working with them. Improve each position on this list. Try to make the best impression during the connection with the client.

For example, in the company Konica Corporation - particular attention was paid to the first visit of potential customers to the office. Their way passed through firm shops the client could imagine, how his shop will look like. The task was to visit the office a pleasant procedure. This had a very positive effect on the desire of potential customers.

All that somehow concerns the client is marketing. So, this is your job.

What if, in your case, the decision making stages last several months? Contact points can be much longer. For example, a potential client could visit your site several times, read several articles, receive 2-3 emails through your mailing list, come across a post with social networks, see 10 times an ad in retargeted advertising and only after that buy something from you It remains to build interaction with potential clients so as to contact them at all stages.

What to do with those who have reached the Buying stage, which brought joy? You have to deal with the product, service, design, and description.

5. How do I influence my purchase decision?

How does the buyer behave when making the final purchase decision? Compares companies, brand services by parameters, as a rule, unconsciously.

Different parameters are important for different customers. Each parameter has "points" that determine its importance for a particular customer. It makes sense to divide your customers into segments - groups - depending on the typical "sets of points."

Imagine the situation, and the buyer wants to buy from your company a "baby bed" for his home, which is a hundred miles from Seattle. For him, the "Delivery" parameter will be more critical than for a person who lives in the city.

The usefulness of the product" table .

Based on this information, it is possible to form a segment on a geographical principle with identical points for parameters from the decision-making matrix.

An example of a decision-making table for a Seattle child's bed customer on a 10-point scale

Parameter

Ease of use of the site -6

Trust in the company -8

Terms of delivery -8

Cost -6

Proximity to home -3

Warranty- 6

Assembly option -3

If the buyer finds six companies with delivery options? He will start to choose from the list of other parameters.

We've come to the critical question.

Which parameter is the most important compared to the competitors? This parameter is "trust in your company, brand"!

6. How content marketing builds customer confidence in your company.

On all sides, we hear "buy!" "buy!" "buy!" Perhaps our brains would explode if people did not have advertising filters. To get through to the client, we need to bypass the filters! The circumvention is done through expert positioning with the help of content marketing.

Trust is a very powerful tool, but it takes a long time to build and confirm in the process of interaction with the client

Do you agree that customers consider people who provide their customers with useful information, articles, guides, videos, experts, and trust them? In my opinion, "trust" is one of the most important arguments when making a purchase. The sooner you start to work with a potential customer, the greater the opportunity to increase the parameter of "trust" in comparison with competitors.

This does not mean that the rest of the parameters from the decision-making table can be neglected. Determine the importance of each of them for your potential customers.

What result to expect?

Based on the results of the "Purchase Stages" and "Decision-Making Tables" with the key parameter "Trust,": content marketing increases the flow of applications and the probability of purchase based on scenarios of potential customers' behaviour in the selection of goods and services. This distinguishes content marketing from merely fashionable technologies and temporary trends.

Content marketing is an electronic superstructure over the actions of potential customers, their behaviour "before" and at the time of purchase.

7. Step-by-step algorithm for launching a content marketing strategy for your business.

Let's take a closer look at what are the main elements of the content marketing strategy of "inbound marketing" and what needs to be done to launch it.

Create expert content interesting for your potential customer's article, video. Could you give them a solution to their request?

Distribute the content to all advertising channels that are in demand among your potential customers.

Repeat regularly points 1 and 2 at least 2-4 times a month. The first requests from potential customers can come at once. However, a serious flow, if you do everything correctly, will start only in 8-14 months.

8. Formalized strategy - "foundation" of content marketing.

Before you start creating content, writing articles, videos, and so on, you need to define the topics and content of your articles. How to do this?

The content marketing strategy written down in the text will help you to do this. It should provide answers to the following key questions:

- Describe a typical portrait of the customer: habits, character, hobbies, interests, values. What are your personal as well as other people's needs and objectives that your potential customer usually solves with your product or service?

- What are the typical objections, fears, and arguments against buying?

- What benefits will he gain from purchasing the product or service? What are the main reasons your potential customer may follow when making a decision? Who can influence his decision? Who really takes it?

It's time to get to work. Open the text editor right now and write down the answers for your company. Wasn't that easy?

Take your time to close. There are several other questions that should be answered before starting work on content marketing.

Content marketing toolset

Where do "tools" come from? Out of the need to perform a set of actions within the framework of the content marketing strategy. A detailed list of actions is provided below, each with its own tool.

Develop a content marketing strategy. Create a foundation for the rest of the tools. The strategy should describe the interests of your potential customers, possible objections, and doubts that prevent the purchase. It has been detailed above.

Expert blog. Use it to publish useful articles, videos, and other information. Provide a potential client with helpful information to launch the "principle of mutual exchange" and "pump up" the trust in your company.

Launch E-mail marketing. Distribute useful articles to potential clients, along with information about your company's services/goods.

Start contextual advertising. Promote your articles through search engine output and advertising networks of search engines.

Activate advertising in social networks. At the right time, in the right place, with the right people to share useful information for them (expert articles, videos, document templates, etc.), get feedback from potential customers.

Whether or not your company should use content marketing now and "take the cream from the market" is up to you.

Chapter 4. Positioning the company.

Marketing without positioning is not effective

The main objective of positioning

There are many versions of positioning, but the author of this concept was the famous Jack Trout. As early as 30 years ago, he said: "That marketing without positioning will not be effective. Jack noted that positioning is how consumers perceive a brand and associate it with specific properties.

When ambitions are higher than opportunities

International companies electronics

It was the case when, before being allowed to participate in the tender. You and the company are checked by all the services. Security service, monitoring service. Financial assistance. We prepared the meeting for about 3 months. The meeting took place. It looked like this, I and the CFO were sitting in the centre, and there was a circle of people around us. About 20 people. I am 25 years old, and in front of us people with 20-25 years of experience in the field of advertising, it was funny, I did not slow down, and demonstrated confidence in the company's strength, giving my guarantees. I also had with me a folder of printed copies of reference sheets, which we received from our favourite customers. We finished on a good note, and I rejoiced in my heart in anticipation of the most significant contract at the time. Two weeks later, we received technical documentation that only met my expectations, but not the company's capabilities. We were sent a contract that had two kinds of cooperation. Option 1, we had to close 270 mega-markets with our services in 150 cities. The amount of the contract was $1,250,000 in less than a year. And option 2, where there were 30 mega-markets in 10 most complex and remote cities.

As a result, this cooperation became an untapped opportunity. I was never upset about it, but I saw how upset the people who had already spent that money in their minds were. I saw it as a confirmation of my expectations and the reality of the moment.

I realized there was no need to punch through the wall or knock on the closed doors, which would always be enough!

1. Winning Brand Positioning Strategies.

Positioning is the first product association and property association.

Colgate - tooth whitening, Blend-a-med - caries protection.

The rest of the trademarks fall into the same category - "the same". That is, you do not understand the differences between them. At the same time, Colgate and Blend-a-med are already positioned in your mind.

That's why it's so important to differentiate yourself from your competitors. But it is even more important that your customers understand these differences. What's more, we knew what benefits they would get. This is the main task of positioning!

Positioning is the development of a proposal and brand image, which are aimed at forming or strengthening the competitive position of the brand in a particular market. Everyone can't position a brand because it blurs the image of the brand. The brand position should be clearly defined and unshaken. The main goal of positioning is to differentiate oneself from competitors and strengthen one's position.

2. Brand positioning concept.

Every company, even if it is a small firm, needs a clear positioning strategy. This is useful for both employees and consumers.

The narrower the niche the brand occupies in the market, the easier it is to plan the strategy. For example, juice production equipment is very specialized, but it has a specific target audience.

Most likely, the clients of such a company appreciate the quality, but do not want to overpay for the equipment. Therefore, equipment suppliers choose price positioning or by the consumer. Unlike equipment, mineral water is used by almost all Ukrainians. In this case, it is difficult to position the brand on the consumer, and water is positioned on the application or benefit: mineral water for those who are engaged in sports or for those who want to become healthier. Positioning helps to emphasize the individuality of the brand.

The first step in brand positioning is to choose the right strategy. Brand competitiveness and loyal customers depend on it.

3. Main brand positioning strategies.

I highlight the main strategies of brand positioning in the market. These strategies will be suitable for new companies as well as for those brands that want to enter a new market or take a bigger share.

1. Competitive positioning

This positioning strategy is based on the brand's opposition to the competitor from whom it is planned to win market share. The brand may be presented as an anti-competitor or superior in quality. Such a brand positioning strategy is used against the market leaders by those companies that occupy the 2nd or 3rd place. Competitive positioning takes into account the weaknesses of the leading company and is based on the unsatisfied desires of consumers.

When choosing this strategy, you should be honest with consumers. The brand should correspond to the declared advantages over the market leader; otherwise, the consumers will not accept it.

Examples

One of the first historical examples of this strategy is the positioning of vehicles as horseless crews.

At one time, the 7ups were aligned with the «Not Cola» strategy from stake producers, including the Coca-Cola. A consumer who does not want to buy a coke will subconsciously choose a neo-cola - 7up.

IBM's slogan is "Think." This has helped Apple to counteract IBM with the phrase "Think different" and positioning computers as those designed for entertainment.

2. Category positioning

When developing brand positioning in a particular category, the marketing campaign focuses on promoting the brand as a leader in a specific product category. This strategy is particularly beneficial when creating a new market. Such positioning will be successful only if the company has one:

an innovative solution for the market;

The product has unique properties;

There is a demand for a new approach to solving the problem.

Examples:

In 1949, Xerox launched the world's first copier, creating a new market. Today, the company continues to hold a leading position in this market, and the word "copier" has become a common word for all copiers.

In 2012, the electric car market was represented by economy segment machines (25-35 thousand dollars). Tesla Motors created a new niche of premium electric vehicles, selling Model S at a price of $75,000 or more. This opened up the electric car market for a large segment.

3. Consumer positioning

The creation of brand positioning by the consumer is recommended in the event that the brand advertising campaign focuses on a specific target audience. This strategy is also suitable for small companies that produce goods with particular properties. In the advertising of such a brand, the product is associated with a particular class of customers, using the phrases "created for...", "for those who...": for example, Lenovo: "For those who do".

Advertising is often carried out with the help of famous personalities, whose image becomes associated with the product.

Examples:

Pepsi's positioning in 1961: "For those who think young." Virginia Slims were positioned as cigarettes exclusively for women.

Linux is positioned as an operating system for IT professionals. Macintosh - as the best personal computer for photographers and designers.

Famous Fixtures brand produces and installs retail equipment for retail chains and, at the same time, is a retailer itself. This helped the company to increase brand credibility because customers understood that the equipment was sold to them by employees in the same industry. Their slogan was "Famous Fixtures - retailer-owned, retailer built, retailer tested.

4. Positioning by benefit

This type of brand positioning can be based on both emotional and rational benefits. Positioning should give a clear answer to the buyer's question, "What do I get from choosing this brand?

This strategy has low efficiency in highly competitive markets, where the proposed benefits quickly lose their relevance as all companies start copying each other.

Examples:

Strong brands are able to implement this strategy even in the large market effectively. Honda and Toyota have focused on the economy and reliability of their machines. Volvo - emphasis on safety and durability.

Crest toothpaste stands out due to the efficiency of caries control, but today this benefit is used by almost all pastes.

Nike often plays on the emotional benefits of consumers. The "Write the future" campaign includes such slogans:

Play to be remembered

Change history with just one strike

Weave your way to immortality

4. Price positioning of the brand.

There are several approaches to this positioning.

1. The same for less cost

Price positioning of the brand as cheap is suitable for companies whose products do not boast a high degree of consumer involvement and which are chosen rationally (lower left sector in the figure). For example, Fast Moving Consumer Goods, which are not of concern to consumers or are expected to be of lower quality, will be purchased at a lower price. A strategy is successful if there are leaders in the market who sell goods at unreasonably high prices.

In this case, the strategy is used primarily for the economy segment of consumers, using similar slogans:

Cheaper only for nothing

Like home, but less expensive.

Windows like everyone else, but cheaper.

If you can't tell the difference, why pay more

2. More for more money

Consumers believe that quality goods should be expensive. At the same time, they buy not only the product itself but also prestige and the opportunity to belong to the category of people "who can afford it."

3. Less for less

Suitable for people who don't want to overpay for what they can do without. For example, Southwest Airlines offers cheap flights, but they do not provide lunch for passengers, and they have uncomfortable lounges.

6. Positioning the application

The brand product is tied to a specific consumption situation. Thus, the consumer will buy exactly this product in a necessary situation. The more unique the situation, the narrower the market, which allows you to take a leading position quickly. At the same time, it is necessary to monitor the hobbies and behaviour of consumers consistently, because their habits may change, and the positioning strategy will quickly become obsolete.

Examples:

The Saab was positioned in Norway as "the best for the Norwegian winter", which helped to increase sales quickly. Coca Cola is like a holiday drink on Christmas Eve.

7. Positioning by attribute

This strategy uses the distinctive characteristics of the brand and is the most common. Positioning does not focus on the differences from competitors, but on the unique properties of the product, which make it special.

Examples:

Application of this strategy by the Schlitz beer brand:

World's largest-selling beer

The beer that made Milwaukee famous

Real gusto in a great light beer

The Pillsbury brand began to position the flour for baking as "flour with ideas," simply putting the recipe in the package. Ready Crisp Bacon was positioned as bacon, which you don't have to worry about - warm it up in the microwave.

8. Positioning prestige

Unlike happiness, prestige is easy to buy - there are always people who are willing to pay for special treatment, the opportunity to be a VIP. Such positioning is suitable for companies that produce genuinely luxurious or premium products. This is not limited to jewellery and expensive cars and can extend to food and everyday goods. There are many stereotypical opinions about prestige:

If a wedding dress, Vera Wang

If the pens, Parker

If the clock, then Rolex

If the perfume, Chanel

If the jewellery, the Tiffany

Prestige can be determined not only by a specific company but also by the whole category. Prestige also means that, for a particular target audience, expensive organic products are available for true vegetarians.

Examples:

This method of brand positioning is used by famous luxury cars:

Maserati - The absolute opposite of ordinary

Bentley - We are opposite of mass production

Porsche - There is no substitute

5. Positioning formula.

Before choosing a positioning strategy, several questions need to be answered.

1. What is your brand? What do you do, and what is your mission?

2. Who is your brand for?

3. What is the need for your brand's products or services?

4. Who are your main competitors?

5. What is your difference from them, and what are your advantages over them?

6. What benefits will your brand bring to the consumer?

With the answers to these questions, it will be easier to choose a strategy that is sure to succeed.

6. What are the benefits of successfully positioning your business?

Developing a brand positioning concept allows you to identify and communicate key brand benefits to your audience. A well-designed communication message forms a positive perception of the product. The main advantage of brand positioning in a competitive niche is the ability to promote the product successfully. Properly drafted communication strategy forms a beautiful image of the company and emphasizes the advantages and competitive advantages of the product. Positioning contributes to the formation of a loyal target audience and strengthening the brand's position in the market.

Thanks to positioning, it is possible to define and formulate brand values, as well as to consolidate stable positive associations among potential customers.

7. Key principles of effective business positioning.

If the company has a quality and exciting product that can solve the problems of the target audience, it is necessary to build a proper communication with potential customers. Positioning will help to bring them information about the competitive advantages of the product and consolidate a positive image of the company. For this marketing tool to work effectively, it is necessary to observe the following key principles:

1) A good product is half the success. If a company has a quality product, it is essential to tell the target audience about it. It is essential to convey information competently, rationally and taking into account the positioning. In this case, it will be possible to form a correct image of the company and the product.

2) Describe how the product is created. Information about the peculiarities of the production of goods and technological processes can become the basis for successful positioning. It is not necessary to tire the target audience with specific terms and complicated explanations, and it is better to attract their attention with the help of interesting and unusual facts.

3) Don't forget the benefits. Successful positioning should attract the attention of potential customers, create a positive image of the company, and stimulate sales. The brand concept cannot be limited to a creative slogan; it is essential to tell about the benefits of the product and the problems it solves.

4) Focus on the product. Some companies try to reach different niches and target audiences. In doing so, the range of products is expanding, and it is challenging to conduct positioning. The company loses its appearance in the eyes of consumers, and it is difficult to distinguish the competitive advantage of the product. It is important to remember that for different groups of consumers, the product has different value and to focus on its target audience.

5) Positioning can be flexible. If the chosen strategy does not bring positive results, it should be changed. In such cases, you can look at the company and the product from a different perspective. It is essential to focus on the benefits and features of the product and brand that have not previously been addressed.

Successful positioning is a long-term strategy. During one advertising campaign, it is impossible to create and fix in the minds of consumers information about the differences between goods and their advantages. Subsequently, the image is strengthened and adapted to different cycles of product life.

The positioning of the company can be tried in an experimental model to be convinced of the effectiveness of this marketing tool. It will help to strengthen the position in the market and effectively develop the business in a highly competitive environment. The main thing to remember is that in positioning, it is vital to keep the promises made to consumers and offer real advantages and benefits.

Show loyalty to the brand, and it will show loyalty to you.

In 2014, we asked a Swiss company, one of the leaders in the field of plant protection and seed production, to participate in an advertising tender. The company is headquartered in Basel, Switzerland. More than 27,000 employees work in 90 countries. Before to receive the possibility to participate in the tender, we have given all the interesting documents, have sent several offers. We have developed unique projects in the direction of marketing and sales increase. The news of this period took about 6 months.

We got the opportunity and started cooperation.

At first, we closed 2 markets with our services, and later we were given all the volume. At that time it was 18 locations of mega-markets in 10 cities.

We successfully fulfilled the contract, which lasted for 6 months with prolongation for another 6 months.

How we found the points of contact and understanding of each other?

At the presentation of the advertising project, we found out for ourselves two precise tasks that face us.

1. To increase brand loyalty in a given area

2. Increase seasonal sales.

I have prepared two options and openly said this in negotiations. The first option is a simple, banal set of advertising cases, which will bring results, but it will be low marginal and cheaper on the budget.

The second option was much more challenging to implement and more expensive. The results could have helped to outperform the competitors locally significantly. To my surprise, the guys from the marketing and advertising department agreed on the second project and expressed their trust.

In this project, our people started working at 07.00 in the morning, and the overall team was about 100 people. The contract was completed and implemented.

Contact points

You should be regularly engaged in points of contact and customer focus in order to create a positive feeling in the buyer. Otherwise, the effectiveness of all marketing campaigns may be compromised.

The client is always right! This is a phrase that company owners use as an example for their employees to teach them good service. The client is always right! It is this phrase that employees hate, believing that they provide good service, and the client behaves improperly.

A fine line between good and bad is called customer focus.

If you have just decided: "In my company, the service is good, and therefore customer-oriented at a high level," I would advise you to take your time. Your service can be good compared to competitors or on average in the market. But we are talking about you. Even if the customer focus in your company is high. The phrase "There is no limit to perfection" will be relevant here.

I'm debunking myths from my point of view. These are the stages I had to go through personally. Personal transformation is the key to the development of the personality as a whole.

1. Tomorrow, Today Will Be Yesterday.

- My company has sales scripts and customer service regulations, and employees are obliged to talk about them, which means my company is client-oriented. No, it is not.

- My company continually measures the Net Promoter Score index, which we have been monitoring for two years now. It means that my company is client-oriented. Not again.

- My company has implemented a customer loyalty program, which costs me a lot of money. So my company is client-oriented. Also, no.

- "I was so well served by the company. I started sending my friends to them. I was also given bonuses for this. That's what I understand about being customer-centric. Getting in at 10!

These quotes now show that business owners consider it to be client-oriented, which is not what it is because clients perceive everything in a very different way.

Therefore, let's immediately define the concept of client-oriented to get rid of false illusions.

Client-centric is the ability to identify the needs of the client and meet them, exceeding his expectations, which will make him happy.

If to disassemble this definition in practical application to business, then client-orientedness is special actions on the "happiness" of clients.

Thanks to which they become loyal to your company, and start not only to buy constantly and more often but also to promote your company among their friends and acquaintances.

2. Plenty of pros and cons.

Any marketing tool was invented for something. And in the very notion of client-oriented, you can see the advantages that it brings to the company.

But "motivating customers to buy more frequently" is just one of the advantages. Let's look at them in more detail.

Increase in a client-oriented approach will positively influence the company because:

A higher chance that customers will come to you for products;

The process of selling the product is greatly simplified;

The client thinks less about the cost of the product;

The outflow of regular customers is minimal;

New clients through warm recommendations

Plus, as you can see, a lot. They are not mythical, but, as they say, they can even be tried on with money.

But like in the saying, there is a spoonful of tar everywhere. And in our case, it's quite significant - it's not easy to become a client-oriented company. I would even say that it is very difficult and I will explain why.

3. Foundation of The Approach.

In order for your service to be rated 5+ and you to receive three Michelin stars (the highest award in the meal), you need to know the fundamental, basic principles of customer-centricity. They are not complicated, but have a great depth:

Clarification, understanding and customer satisfaction;

Comfortable communication with consumers, built on trust and respect for each other;

Realization of products that meet the expectations of consumers, and even better, exceed them;

The willingness of the company's management to communicate in case of positive and negative references;

The flexibility of the organization to change in the wake of changes in consumers and their desires.

To summarize all this, it will be possible to create a strategy based on service and feedback to retain customers.

This is all you need to know about the concept before you move on to specific tools to increase customer focus.

4. Small business does not need service?

The only thing I would like to pay attention to is who is suitable for a client-oriented approach.

That is, what company needs to be purposefully engaged in it and whom better to postpone for later and to engage in the attraction of clients.

Yes, now there are many rumours that it is necessary only for those who work in highly competitive niches. Small companies, monopolists, and innovative startups do not need it. But this is a mistake, or rather an excuse not to engage in this business.

Monopolists can "score" on good service only for the time being until a new competitor appears.

Then dissatisfied customers will immediately go to him. A startup has a much better chance of a "powerful start" due to good service, external and internal customer orientation.

Small businesses should appreciate each client as the apple of its eye, not to make ends meet in sales endlessly, and run a warm recommendation.

Therefore, it is necessary for everyone. Only one question - "To what extent? This is becoming more and more flexible.

There is no point in killing yourself over just one service. People will not go for one service only. Therefore, it is like in the design of sites; you need to do well, but not perfect. After all, the work on the ideal - endless.

5. Two Types of Approach.

You could say we started talking about practice. For its basis, we need to divide the customer focus into two types, which many do not guess about.

They can be conventionally defined as external and internal client-oriented.

Client-centric employee (internal)

The customer focus of the staff is a huge plus. These are very valuable employees who are quite expensive in the labour market.

They differ not only in that they comply with all the regulations on communication with the client, but also in the fact that "the main focus" is not on the company and management, and the client.

Although it sounds strange, the example is as old as the world, but it reflects the idea most fully.

It is they who follow the proverb: "You are paid by the client, not the manager.

It is challenging to evaluate and see such employees, but as a rule, they are good sales managers selling much more of their colleagues. It is they who have the most loyal and loyal customers.

A client-oriented company is an external

It is a company primarily focused on long-term work and long-term business presence.

For this purpose, the company develops whole rules, regulations, and scripts of communication between employees and clients. Where is it written even what temperature to pour tea to the client?

Checklists are good, but it is impossible to foresee all situations. Therefore, the company's management should initially define the strategy not only to create the rules but also to nurture this attitude in each employee.

Unfortunately, this is the most important problem, because companies are more focused on money and customers, and not on working with employees.

6. Examples of Successful Solutions.

A clothing store. In case the client needs a different size in the locker room, all he needs to do is press the button, which will signal the seller and bring the required size.

Usually, the customer has to shout or, worse, dress in his clothes and repeat the circle of honour.

Center for Child Development. Administrators of the company give out tablets with the Internet and games for those parents who are waiting for their child during the class.

Thus, time flies by unnoticed, and all this is supported by comfortable and large armchairs.

Starbucks Coffee House. They write your name on every cup of coffee ordered. This helps them not only to find the owner of the drink but also to communicate with the customer by name all the time. And as you know, we are ready to listen to our name forever.

Jewellery "Cartier". For all popular countries on place, carriers of language are given. And for rare countries, you can be provided with an interpreter for a few hours.

Restaurant pizza. Since the restaurant is very famous, with the influx of season, there are queues for tables that go along the street.

The waiting time can be up to 1 hour. To ensure that you are not tired, you are provided with chairs and free water, which is continuously replenished by the waiter in this area.

Taxi service. When ordering a car, you can choose the option "Silent driver".

Such an order will make it clear to the taxi driver that you need to go silently. For many customers, this is a significant aspect

7. How Does A Skills Manager Act?

It is impossible to give a list of mandatory actions to become a customer-oriented company.

You have already understood that all criteria are based on the needs of the client.

In one business, the consumer needs to have interactive television in the queue, and the other, that this queue would be as fast as possible.

The third category of people will say that you need interactive television and a fast turn. The company will answer all these requests; the main thing is that everyone should choose rationally from the height of their capabilities.

If we are talking about small and medium-sized businesses, then all the resources and time are not available.

Therefore, it is necessary to move on the priority and start with the most important. Here are a few practical tips that will help you to form the right actions to lay the foundations of customer focus.

1. Determine the direction. Mostly you are focused on the client or money. This is important because, for example, customers are often dissatisfied with the product and demand an exchange, gift, and refund.

By law, in some cases, you can refuse them. But the fact is that customer focus is not the law, so you need to decide what to do from the start.

2.Give the client more than he or she expects. "Easy to say, but difficult to do" - you think. But in fact, it is not.

For example, all a retailer needs to do is put a chocolate bar in a customer's purchase. This will surprise him and ruin you for a penny.

3.Do not collect feedback through questionnaires. This is a serious mistake.

Questionnaires do not work, because even a positive client is lazy to fill it out, and if he does, he writes only good things so as not to offend.

4.Count the outflow of clients. Clients leave, and this cannot be avoided. But if the clients leave everything, you need to change something urgently.

After all, the outflow of customers is one of the indicators of your service.

5.Communicate with angry or gone customers. Be ready to talk to the lost client at any time.

The powerful effect is achieved if the issue is solved not just by an employee, but by his manager. And it will brighten up the negative if the problem has not been resolved positively.

6.Work out a motivation system for employees. Introduce bonuses to the best client-oriented employees; it will be an additional incentive for them.

The prize can be either material or non-material, as long as the employee wants it.

Calculation Formula

Everybody knows a lot about the client-oriented approach, but there is no single formula that takes into account all factors.

An interesting study by Ovum is a large research centre.

They have developed their formula and decided to test different companies to see which one is customer-centric. Ready for the results?

Even such large companies as Apple, IBM, General Electric could not rise above 80%. The absolute majority of companies have not even crossed the bar above 55%.

This perfectly shows that most companies do not "bother" with the quality of work. But somehow, it is necessary to count? For this purpose, we can use the approach of assessing the consumer loyalty index.

Only by sharpening the questions for service and quality of service in order to avoid the reduction of the coefficient due to the product and other technical aspects that are not directly related to customer focus.

Inside from the world of marketing

According to rumours and unverified information, when one large country opened the first IKEA in the capital. Documentation, regulations, business processes, etc., were brought 10 trucks, 2 of which were occupied by customer communication documentation.

Therefore, I would like to emphasize that a customer-oriented company is not established quickly. For a small business, internal and external customer orientation is also relevant, but in a smaller format.

Besides, the task is to focus not on chips, but the basic points. In order to do everything correctly and not to confuse the focus, I act according to the following plan:

1. I determine the points of contact with the client;

2. I build them into the list by priority;

3. Continually improve after feed-back client.

This is a continuous effort to improve, but there is a "cost of living" and here to determine whether you have reached it or not, look at the number of lost customers, and the number of satisfied.

If the overall picture is not frightening, you are moving in the right direction. Let slowly but surely.

8. 10 keys to be aware of when working with clients.

You now have a translation of the results of a number of studies on social psychology conducted in the United States. Read and be aware of what customers want.

1. Buyers prefer good service to fast

15 minutes in heaven is better than five minutes in hell. According to recent research, customers who have received a competent, professional, and detailed service are more likely to remember you and tell your friends about you. In addition, buyers named rough, fussy and incompetent service as the first reason not to turn to the services of such a company. Thus slow service does not cause such adverse reaction.

2. Buyers love individual approach and are ready to pay for it

In the study of the Journal of Applied Social Psychology, participants were able to increase the average number of tips received by waiters by 23% without changing the quality of service. They were able to achieve this result when they began to bring a second set of chewing gum after they brought a check. Waiters who only brought gum once received 7% less tip.

3. Buyers will remember you if you know them by name

Nothing gives such a wonderful feeling of sympathy as an e-mail with gratitude for the purchase.

Speaking of a personal approach, according to recent brain activity research, only a few sounds are as pleasing to us as the sound of our name. People indeed become much more attentive and interested when they hear their name. So make sure that your company takes advantage of the benefits of personalized customer service whenever possible.

4. Nothing causes as much excitement as a nice little thing to buy

One of the most memorable (and therefore discussed) moments in the consumer experience is a pleasant surprise. Feedback, especially unexpected feedback, is power! For example, Zappos regularly spoils its customers with free delivery the day after the purchase to make them feel good.

5. Creating a good customer relationship doesn't have to cost you a lot

Since the launch of the Unexpected Sweet Gifts campaign, the business has grown by 300% annually. The concept of "Frugal WOWs" is especially important for small companies. Creating good relationships with customers depends on what you do and pay a little.

The founder of the restaurant chain Sweet green N.R. often sends his employees to arrange restaurant coupons on the windshields of parked cars.

With these surprises, the firm achieves a significant increase in customer loyalty.

6. If customers at least once use your loyalty program, they will continue to use it further

Consumer psychologists at Dreze & Nunes, in their well-known study of the car wash industry, have found out how consumers are becoming committed to loyalty programs. The researchers have demonstrated that consumers are twice as likely to remain in a loyalty program if the program has already been launched by the time they join: tasks that are in the process of being completed are more likely to be completed.

7. Buyers love brand stories, and their use in sales has proven effective

We can say about stories - the further they are told, the more they are believed. A study by Melanie Green and Timothy Brack found that a good story is the most persuasive form of oral and written communication.

They believe that this is because history can "move" us to another space, which allows the brand to leave a powerful (and memorable) mark in the memory of the buyer.

8. If you love everything innovative, your customers can be a great source of inspiration for you

Eric von Hippel of MIT conducted a joint study with the Institute of Science Management on the relationship between "leading consumers" and innovation in companies. A study of 1193 commercially successful innovations in 9 different industries found that 60% of them came from consumers.

9. Sell time, not money, and your customers will appreciate your brand

Most people think that the best indicator of who they are in the way they spend their time, not the amount of money spent on a particular thing. It makes sense why popular beer brands advertise good pastime rather than low prices. A recent study by Stanford University found that customers have better feelings for a brand they associate with "having a good time," memories of a good time are better remembered than memories of good prices.

10. If you use the image of money in advertising, customers become more selfish

According to a study by psychologists, when the image of money is broadcast to customers in an advertising campaign, they become more selfish and less able to help others. This property can be used by companies selling luxury goods that can benefit from images associated with charitable and gratuitous aid to others in advertising.

9.How to give a discount without a discount.

Dan Kennedy always has a lot of chips in his arsenal. I want to tell you about one of them today. Dan Kennedy himself calls this method "discount without discount".

"I made millions of dollars on cassettes with a training system for doctors at evening seminars; the seminars were free of charge, but the doctors had to deposit $25 to ensure that they would come. The deposit was returned at the end of the seminar. After the commercial presentation and the closing of the sales, I was making this sale of the price. I was saying: well, you can take your deposit ($25), which guaranteed that you would be here tonight. Since you kept your promise, your $25 will return to you. And we can double your return. You can deduct $50 if you buy a training system tonight. Its price is $499 minus $50. Even in an auditorium where many people were arguing with this problematic strategy, it worked magically. I put $50 in their pockets and then throw it in the fire. If they don't buy the system, they lose $50, which is painful! Think about how you can use this technique in your business, what you can sell for a lower price and then sell for a higher price.

10. The effect of free.

We all know how much the magic word affects us for free. But not many people use this effective tool to attract customers. Why is it so profitable to give something for free?

To answer this question, I will talk about an experiment conducted by Dan Ariely, the author of the book "Behavioral Economics." Dan Ariely has decided to test how the free offer can affect a person's actions and choices. At one of the universities, Dan set up a table with expensive chocolate truffles and regular candy. At the same time, he set prices well below the market average. The famous Swiss truffles cost only 15 cents, and the lollipop cost 1 cent. As expected by the experimenters, the winner was the truffle, which was preferred by 73% of buyers.

Then Dan decided to change the terms of the experiment, reducing the price of both candies by 1 cent. At the same time, truffles began to cost 14 cents, while lollipops - 0 cents. It would seem that the price was reduced equally by 1 centner, and, accordingly, the preferences of customers should not have changed. Truffles continued to be sold at a very attractive price.

But the results of the experiment have changed dramatically. This time, only 31% of buyers preferred truffles, while free lollipops were 69%. The effect was free.

Why does the free effect have such a strong impact on people? To find the right answer to this question, it is necessary to immerse yourself in the psychology of the person, namely to look at his fears. One of the strongest fears is the fear of loss. When we pay for something, we are afraid that we might make the wrong choice. Thus, we have a hard time with money or other things. When we face free of charge, the fear of loss disappears, because there is nothing to lose. That's why the effect of free is so strong. Seeing the free offer, our consciousness refuses to assess all the disadvantages and possible consequences. That's why we make unnecessary purchases so often. Now you won't be surprised why supermarkets regularly hold promotions: "Buy X units - get 1 more free of charge as a gift.

Those who work hard are given opportunities!

The first project with this company, I have earned 10 USD per month. In the next 16 months, the contract amount was 600 000$.

It is a giant company in the book market, which sells its products in more than 30 countries.

Once my sales department gave me a client who needed services in the field of BTL advertising recruiting. The request for cooperation implied a pilot project. After completing the task, I proposed. It was a developed project in the direction of attracting new customers, a clear sales plan, and a bonus for the fulfilled conditions. Geography on 72 cities, with coverage of 112 trading platforms. This plan was approved, and soon the companies began to give the opportunity to prove themselves. First of all, 5 cities, then 10, and so on and so on. The project was successfully implemented and completed in due time. Each of your old clients is always ready to listen, and 50% are ready to buy again.

Chapter 6. The Old Client Is 5 Times More Valuable Than New.

You have to be in charge of client retention. After all, the cost of attracting a new customer will cost you at least 5 times more. And selling to an old client is much easier because he is already familiar with you.

The marketing policy, as a rule, is directed on the decision of several kinds of problems, one of which is the formation of the loyal client relation to a brand and the offered goods. In general, loyalty is characterized as building long-term relationships with customers, customers or consumers. A side effect of such a policy is the increase in the company's profit. According to statistics, it is enough to think over the steps to retain regular customers, and the profit will increase significantly. If the retention coefficient increases by 5%, the average cost of purchases increases by 20% to 99%. It becomes interesting at once! However, this trend is observed only in one case: if the company is not only following the economic indicators but also builds its ideology.

Over time, this reduces the cost of marketing and advertising campaigns. Increasing customer loyalty is a long-term task that requires an individual approach. Before introducing concrete steps in this direction, it is necessary to think over the program in general, to develop the primary purposes, and to co-ordinate ways of their realization. How to increase customer loyalty, what steps to take?

1. Loyalty program for the client "Let's be friends."

Even if the buyer comes only for a service or a certain product, he has multiple needs: in entertainment, to eliminate problems, to realize desires, to get emotions. All these tasks must be solved by marketing.

Sometimes newcomers in business are focused only on attracting the primary client audience, but it is much cheaper and more effective to turn to secondary sales. This allows not only to influence the target audience but also to transfer customers to the rank of permanent.

Loyalty programs are aimed at this result. In order to increase customer loyalty, we should not forget about the interaction with the customer base, based on which we develop unique offers, individual discounts, and gifts.

Creating customer loyalty programs includes such components:

- Thinking over the general strategy, selection of marketing tools;

- Calculation of the average check of regular customers;

- Formation of unique offers;

- Informing about the launch of the loyalty program;

- Connection of regular customers;

- The functioning of programs and further development.

2. How to increase customer loyalty.

Marketers, advertisers, managers are thinking about the answer to this question. Since loyalty presupposes trust, friendly attitude of the client to the brand or store, it is formed based on two components:

- financial;

- psychological, emotional.

The first criterion is provided using traditional methods: discounts, sales, discount cards, bonus schemes, savings discounts, cache backs.

It is more challenging to make it so that consumers get moral satisfaction and positive emotions related to the point of sale or brand. Storytelling, mailing, surprises, and gifts are used for this purpose.- active use of gaming, which is focused on the formation of psychological mood.

Two more factors play an essential role: the level of service and after-sales support. If they are at a low level, do not meet the requirements of clients, it is almost impossible to achieve a positive attitude.

I practised and applied the following methods to form customer loyalty:

- Providing discounts, both general and personal;

- Introduction of bonus and accumulation systems;

- Issuance of loyalty cards, opening of individual accounts;

- Formation of the customer base on the basis of filled in questionnaires, purchase history, personal profiles in social networks;

- Improvement of personnel service level, development of the individual approach to the target audience, selection of effective tools for each client.

The transition to a two- or three-stage scheme of work is reasonable and effective:

- The first level manager makes a "cold call," establishes communication with representatives of the target audience - this is the beginning of cooperation, during which the potential customer receives information about the store or brand. At this stage, the probability of making a purchase is 5-20%;

- The second-tier manager is in contact with customers who have already made purchases. At this stage, consumers are introduced to the assortment of goods, new products, the accompanying last purchase of products;

- As managers of the first and second levels continue to search for and attract new customers, regular customers may feel "abandoned." Here the third level managers are included in the game, the task of which is to continue communication with the client to fix cooperation with the shop.

At the last stage, it is expedient to include the client in the loyalty program, to convince to fill in questionnaires, to get a cumulative or bonus card. Having made two purchases in the store or used the services twice, the client has already made an idea about the point of sale or the company. During this period, it is open for cooperation, and the moment should be used to increase customer loyalty. Otherwise, a person may go to the competitors; you will have to take steps to return the client. This is more difficult than initially keeping it (both in terms of finance and time).

Answering the question of how to increase customer loyalty, we must not forget that goods and services must be of high quality and the corresponding cost. Two aspects should be emphasized once again: the polite approach to each customer and after-sales service. These are two "whales," on which the loyal attitude of the client audience is based; without them, no steps will bring results. Different methods are used to solve such issues:

-Training for the staff, training to communicate with clients;

-Brand beeches, which describe the legend, history, and concept of the brand or company;

- Constant control, the involvement of "mystery shoppers" - such steps allow you to monitor the behaviour of staff, to identify problems in this area;

- Regular professional development of employees, timely training.

As for after-sales service, this approach has a practical use: customers do not look for third-party services, again addressing already familiar managers. In addition, a careful attitude to the customer who made the purchase forms a positive perception of the company or store in his eyes.

To increase this effect, the loyalty program includes additional services. This may be an opportunity to use bonuses for the purchase of related products, gifts in the form of coupons for maintenance and repair of products purchased earlier.

3. Stages of loyalty development.

To choose ways for the decision of this question follows at the formation of a business, simultaneously with working out of an advertising campaign which is directed on the acquaintance of the consumer with the goods. At this time, the basics of loyalty to the target audience, the trust of a particular brand are laid. It is necessary to think over the strategy which the company will follow.

Immediately after the attraction of the buyer, begin actions to increase his loyalty. This allows us to interact individually in the future, to use effective tools for a particular customer, to develop unique offers. Such steps change the psychological mood of the buyer, provide positive emotions, which are the basis for high sales.

4. 8 Steps of the loyalty program for the client "Let's be friends."

I propose to systematize the stages of customer loyalty development in this order:

1) The initial acquaintance of the target audience with the company, product, trademark, store is an advertising campaign aimed at brand recognition;

2) Formation of the idea of the value system, company's guidelines, shop, trademark - here consumers "try on" a product or service, make the first impression about them;

3) Persuasion to make a purchase - as a result of a cold call, click on a link found by a key request, etc.

4) Making the first purchase;

5) Contact with the manager or representative of the company, who offers related products, expresses the pleasure of meeting a new customer;

6) Regular communication with managers, second purchase;

7) Offer to take part in the bonus program, to register, to subscribe to the mailing list, to the profile of the company or the store in social networks;

8) Development of individual proposals, the formation of closer cooperation with the client.

At the last stage, it is worthwhile to establish consumer awareness and effectively use mobile phone applications.

5. Formation of customer loyalty in general.

Modern companies pay considerable attention to this issue. With a client-oriented approach, resources are invested in attracting consumers and meeting their needs. It allows achieving the transition of clientele to the category of constant.

Firms and stores that implement customer-centric methods get advantages over competitors. Their customers buy both familiar services or goods and novelties. In addition, they create a positive image of the company, leaving positive feedback about it, telling friends or acquaintances. This is one of the most effective methods of free advertising.

Forming customer loyalty has such advantages:

1) Consumers are more tolerant of fluctuations in the cost of goods

2) Remain loyal to the brand or brand, even in case of price increases or crisis.

3) The cost of their purchases is significantly higher than that of single or "casual" consumers.

In order to take advantage of such advantages, one should first form a loyal attitude and attract the attention of the target audience.

When building such a process, which is beneficial to both the company and its customers, first of all, it is necessary to proceed from the life cycle of the consumer in the context of the company. On its basis, it is possible to build a "loyalty pyramid" with complementary phases. It generally consists of the above-described stages of customer loyalty development.

1) Initially, marketing activities should be aimed at forming a positive image of the product. It is about branding, developing a legend, or informing customers about the brand. It gives the chance to position the manufacturer or the seller from the necessary side, allows to generate a positive image.

This stage is the first step in forming a friendly and trusting attitude of consumers.

2) The next step is to reveal the advantages that customers get from cooperation with the company. Marketing communications are actively used here, and it is better to do it comprehensively. It is necessary to tell the target audience about the manufacturer (seller) and the product, unique features, and benefits. It should also be emphasized that the service or product offered is the most optimal in terms of quality and cost.

3) It is essential to pay attention to the reality of the stated slogans and messages made in advertising. This allows you to attract new customers and retain existing ones.

4) To ensure the loyal attitude of clients to the company, pay attention to "acquaintance" with them. The process includes studying the target audience, creating a client base, and analyzing purchases made earlier. It allows to individualize the approach and forms the positive psychological mood of the buyer, causes pleasant emotions.

The increase in customer loyalty in the modern market is a guarantee of stable profit and systematic growth of sales. To achieve this goal, use a set of marketing and advertising tools that affect consumer psychologically and financially.

You should regularly work to improve the quality of your products and services! No marketing can save products and services of low quality!

Product quality improvements

The quality of products in modern economic conditions has become the most important factor in competitiveness. It is natural that at market relations, the manufacturer aspires to achieve a stable quality of the production, to use all tools developed by the world and domestic practice. The most important of them is the quality system.

The quality system is a symbiosis of responsibility, processes, and resources that ensures overall quality management.

1. Life and product development stages.

The nature of the impact at the stage of the product life cycle in the quality system is divided into three areas:

1) Formation of quality;

2) Quality management;

3) Quality improvement.

The quality formation is the volume of planned and systematically carried out actions for the implementation of each stage of excellence.

Quality management includes the methods and activities of a prompt response. These include process management, identification of various types of deficiencies in products, production, and elimination of these deficiencies and their causes.

Quality improvement is a continuous activity aimed at improving the quality of products, reducing its costs, and improving production.

The object of the quality improvement process can be any element of production.

For example:

- Technological process

- Introduction of scientific organization of work

-Introduction of modern equipment,

- New marketing tools

- Staff development

- The improvement in quality is directly related to the increase in the competitiveness of products.

The company's management develops and determines the quality policy, ensures integration with other activities, and controls its implementation.

2. «Quality guidelines».

I came to that question the following way.

The main document I used in the development and implementation of the quality system was the brief "Guide to Quality," in which I set out the following data:

1) Regulatory and technological documentation,

2) Product standards

3) Documents confirming the quality of products

The "Quality Guide" can be used as a demonstration material to demonstrate the effectiveness of the quality system.

It can be used to familiarize consumers with the quality system. Marketing and sales department. And also an ordinary employee, for a better understanding of the products.

3. Key product quality indicators.

Quality is a complex philosophical category covering almost all spheres of human activity. The concept of quality includes three elements: object, characteristics, requirements.

The first element is the quality object, which can be a product, product, service, process, organization or individual, or any combination of these. An example of such a combination is the three-dimensional quality of life property.

The second quality element is the characteristics. Goods and services have a set of revealing properties - characteristics. Characteristics can be qualitative.

For example, the smell and taste of food, politeness, and professionalism of the seller, and quantitative; the speed of the car, durability, reliability, and others.

The third element is the requirements. A requirement is, first of all, a manifestation of needs. There is a hierarchy of needs. It is based on basic necessities. Like such things as food, clothing, housing, safety, comfort and convenience of use, aesthetic and social needs.

The top of the pyramid is the need for creativity and self-expression.

4. Product life cycle. Quality system.

The quality system should meet the following basic principles:

- personal participation and responsibility of the manager is to work on product quality assurance;

- distribution of responsibility and authority for each type of activity ensuring implementation of the Company's plan in the field of quality;

- budgeting for product quality assurance;

- ensuring the safety of products, works, services for the consumer and the environment;

- stimulating the development of quality improvement activities;

- improvement of methods and means of quality control.

I hope this information was not too boring for you.

5. Governing Board. Process creators. System holders.

I will divide successful managers into two types; they are equal and cannot develop and be in harmony without each other. The first type is the people "process creators." Creative people are those who are the first to rush to implement complex projects, new projects, and risky projects. There are many billionaires and millionaires among them, but there are also even more bankruptcies. These are people who are creators; their essence is to take up the challenge first of all for themselves. They play well, create new projects, learn quickly, and, most importantly, they can achieve recognition and success in any business.

The second type is "system holders." These are people who have a predominant mathematical beginning. They are very good at counting; they are always collected; they are calculating. They say that these people have a good understanding of other people. It's like they're scanning what's in front of them. This type of scanner is perfect for SEO level directors, CFOs. They become successful investors and businessmen.

I wrote this in order to leave my HR recommendation on recruitment to the marketing and sales departments, as well as to form focus groups in general. After all, the efficiency of the team player is in the right place, the key to success in the team game called "business."

Chapter 8. Knowing Your Client.

I see more and more global examples of CEOs living modestly by possible standards. They want to be like a client, feel like a client, take care of them, and satisfy their needs. What's worth the example of the Amazon campaign? This is a global example of the market reorientation from the principle of "earning" to the principle of "satisfying the need."

You need to know your buyer: his level of income, habits, motives for buying. Otherwise, all your marketing campaigns may fly past your target audience.

In order to understand the global level of attitude to customers of the world's top companies, we will consider specific examples.

1. Examples Of Successful Solutions.

Two main categories are trademarks - trademarks and brands of financial and other services.

The rating was based on information from various open sources, including official company information, media reports, and opinions of industry experts.

I tried to show wide regional geography of the companies and at the same time to show a wide range of industries.

Here are my top, interesting solutions, and customer-oriented companies.

2. Company: Avon.

Industry: cosmetics

Origin: Avon was founded in the USA in 1886.

Avon, a company for women, is a leading international company, internationally recognized expert in the field of beauty. The company's annual sales exceed $5.5 billion. As the largest direct-selling company, Avon offers its services to women in more than 70 countries through millions of independent sales representatives. The company's product range includes perfumes, decorative and care products, jewellery, and clothing.

Avon's history dates back to 1886 when David McConnell founded California Perfume and launched the first product, the Little Dot Perfume Set. The company is rapidly developing, expanding its geographical boundaries.

In 1939, David McConnell, Jr., son of the founder, renamed the company Avon after the English city of Stratford-on-Avon (Stratford-on-Avon), where William Shakespeare, the father's favourite writer, was born. However, the name and logo of Avon were first used in the cosmetics line back in 1929.

In 2019, Avon announced the new Stand4her platform, which aims to improve the lives of 100 million women around the world every year until 2030.

3. Company: Danone.

Industry: fresh dairy and plant-based products, water, baby food, and medical nutrition

Origin: Danone was founded in Spain in 1919.

The history of Danone began in 1919 in Barcelona. Pharmacist Isaac Carasso, using cultures from the Institute of Pasteur and the works of Ilya Mechnikov, created a yoghurt for his son. The boy's name was Daniel. And in the family, Danone. In 1919, Isaac Carasso started selling yoghurt in pharmacies.

In one of the large companies producing water filters, the "Quality Certificate" has been developed and implemented.

He confirmed that the "quality system" works, and this helps to increase the competitiveness of the company. We were engaged in direct marketing for this campaign. We brought people on a production excursion, where they could get acquainted with the "quality certificate" and personally check the information they were interested in. The project was so successful that it was used for more than three years. This had an outstanding impact on the liquidity of the goods on the shelf.

The quality data should be recorded to confirm that the required quality has been achieved. All quality elements should be subject to continuous and regular checks and improvements.

For over 100 years, the Danone Group has been producing healthy and delicious food products adapted to the nutritional needs of consumers. Danone's four business lines - fresh dairy and plant-based products, water, baby food, and medical nutrition - are united by a single principle of work: to offer innovative products of high quality that meet the expectations of consumers at every stage of their lives.

4. Company: Lenovo.

Industry: computers and data centre solutions

Origin: Lenovo was founded in China in 1984.

Lenovo Company was founded on November 1, 1984, by a group of Chinese engineers headed by Liu Chuanzhi. The whole staff consisted of 11 employees. Liu Chuanzhi opened the doors to the world of IBM computers for China. The first innovation in 1985 was the invention of a printed circuit board to adapt hieroglyphics. In 1990 the first personal computer Legend Q286 was released in 1993 - the first PC in China based on Intel Pentium 586 processor, in 1995 - the first server, in 1996 - the first laptop.

Inventions of a team of engineers were ahead of time, setting the vectors of development.

Now Lenovo is a technological giant with offices in 160 countries. Many patents for inventions and technologies indicate the desire for innovation. For example, in 2018, the company patented a flexible laptop, as well as the use of block chain technology to verify the authenticity of documents.

A telling fact: from the first day of existence of the International Space Station of Astronauts NASA was accompanied by a laptop Lenovo ThinkPad A31. Ultra-durable, ultra-productive, and truly legendary line of business laptops ThinkPad tested for compliance with 12 military standards of the U.S. Department of Defense, working in the cold, in heat, resistant to moisture and fires. Lenovo conducts more than 200 internal tests to ensure that customers are confident that this notebook is not afraid of extreme conditions. The company is true to the motto "Infinitely forward" and is not going to stop.

5. Company: Mercedes-Benz.

Industry: vehicles

Localization: All-Ukrainian distribution network

Origin: The Mercedes brand was founded in Germany in 1900.

The history of the Mercedes-Benz brand is based on the stories of two well-known German automobile companies: Benz&Cie. (founded by Carl Benz in 1883)

And Daimler-Motoren-Gesellschaft (founded by Gottlieb Daimler in 1890). Both companies developed independently until 1926, when they merged into a single concern Daimler-Benz, later renamed into Daimler AG.

In 1900, Daimler's Austrian co-owner Emil Jellinek founded a company in Monaco to sell Daimler cars and ordered 36 vehicles, provided that he was given exclusive rights to distribute them in Austria-Hungary, France, Belgium, and the United States under the name Mercedes - named after his daughter. So was born one of the most famous world car brands. She was registered in 1902.

"The best or nothing! - The best or nothing! This is an example of a company that is going to meet the needs of its customers, and I would say, perfectionist and successful person.

6. Company: MetLife.

Industry: Insurance

Origin: MetLife was founded in the United States in 1868.

In 1863, the National Union Life and Limb Insurance Company were founded by a group of New York-based businessmen. Five years later, it was renamed Metropolitan Life Insurance Company, abbreviated MetLife. On March 24, 1868, MetLife signed its first contracts under a new name. The Manhattan office at the time consisted of two rooms, which was sufficient for six employees.

MetLife is now the largest life insurance company in the United States, with operations in more than 40 countries, half of which have leading positions in the insurance market

MetLife's principles - its interest in the well-being and prosperity of its customers, and its willingness to be around in difficult times - reflect MetLife's motto: "Traveling together!

7. Company: Nokian Tyres.

Industry: production and sales of tires

Origin: Nokian Tyres was founded in Finland in 1988.

Finnish company Nokian Tyres is the world's northernmost producer of car tires and one of the most environmentally responsible companies in the industry. Nokian Tyres is known all over the world as the leader of advanced technologies and the inventor of the world's first winter tire. Nokian tires.

Nokian Tyres was founded in 1988, but its roots go back to 1898 when Suomen Gummitehdas - Finnish Rubber Plant was founded in Helsinki. Initially, it produced rubber footwear and various rubber products. In 1904, the company Suomen Gummitehdas opened a factory in Nokia, which became its main production.

At first, it produced rubber footwear, then bicycle tires, and then car tires. In 1934, the plant introduced the world's first winter tire for trucks Kelirengas, and in 1936 the production of legendary winter tires Nokian Nakkareliitta began.

The main task of the research and development department of Nokian Tyres is to develop tires for driving in severe weather conditions. More than half of the costs are incurred in vivo testing at the test site opened in 1986 in Ivalo, Finland's Lapland, 300 km beyond the Arctic Circle. It is impossible to achieve the desired results by testing only in the laboratory. Therefore, it is also carried out in the extreme conditions of the Arctic, and these tires enjoy the well-deserved recognition of customers from around the world and are characterized by logical and predictable behaviour in all situations.

8. *Raise your client - become a client.*

"Many people start enthusiastically without clear boundaries or plans. They follow their dreams, which move them. But they forget that to become a great professional, they first need to become a little professional.

An important step in your client's portrait.

Failure to understand your target audience is one of the worst marketing mistakes.

Such companies first produce products or launch the service, and only then begin to think about who will buy it. To get there for sure, these companies provide universal miracle products "100 in 1", designed for everyone. It is impossible to be everything for everyone. There is such a story that in the office of the company, Procter & Gamble on the walls hang pictures of typical buyers of the company's products with a brief description of each "Jane Smith, 36 years old, secondary education, three children of preschool age. She makes purchases at Wal-Mart and likes to watch

The Oprah Winfrey Show If such large corporations are engaged in the analysis of their customers, why shouldn't you do it for your company?

In order to identify your target audience, you need to correctly identify the desires, needs, experiences, and problems of your customers. Your products and services must be an indispensable solution to help your customers achieve what they want. With such products or services, the issue of attracting customers will not be on the agenda at all.

9. Unique selling proposition – USP.

Unique selling proposition. Recall that in 1961, the famous American advertiser Rosser Reeves wrote the book "The Reality of Advertising. This book has made a revolution in marketing and advertising. But his concept of the need for a unique selling proposition is still valid.

If the buyer does not understand what your offer is profitable for him, he begins to choose the cheapest offer from all existing ones. His choice may not be in your favour. So test your offer.

In order to better understand the essence and concept of USP, I suggest you study examples of already existing successful trade offers.

Food Supermarket Chain (Usa, Europe)

Sell food and basic necessities.

The task was to increase the maximum coverage of customers. I am entering new target groups. Sale of essential goods even to those who are restricted in their movements.

The joint solution was to provide electric scooters to move people with disabilities and the elderly around the supermarket. People with disabilities and the elderly are restricted in their movements, and many of them have almost forgotten what it is to go to a supermarket and choose from a vast number of products. This supermarket allowed them to feel like full-fledged people again!

As a result, all disabled and elderly people who have the opportunity to get to the shops became regular customers of the network. The general public has become more loyal to the company. This innovation has made it more oriented towards the audience that not all companies think about.

Pillow manufacturing company. Australia

The goal was to increase sales by 25-30%. Solution - each pillow has an expiration date in the form of a stamp. The idea that pillows are not eternal was launched into society. An advertising campaign was organized. On television, before bedtime, they showed advertisements about what was going on inside the old pillows at the micro-level.

In the morning, the key words came out of the TV: "Good morning! Did you sleep well? Didn't you wake up the ecosystem in your pillow?" followed by the problem and how to solve it.

The manufacturer showed the problem and suggested solutions. People have been using their pillows for decades. During this time, an entire ecosystem of bacteria that feed on human organisms settles there. People received shocking information from the company, which exposed the pressing problem and at the same time, the way to solve it. The company was the only one who put the shelf life on their pillows. And still, you often notice the expiration date on the pillows?

Sales results surpassed expectations and increased by 300%

Shoe Shop For The Whole Family

High-quality shoes at average prices. Standard medium business.

The standard task is to increase the number of customers, to stand out among competitors, to increase profits.

The solution was to place an electronic flat foot identifier in the store. With the help of advertising to invite people for free to check whether they have or do not have flat feet. If there is, recommend specific shoes.

As a result, the flow of customers increased by 5 times. The number of loyal customers on secondary purchases has increased by 3 times.

Umpqua Holdings Corporation, d.b.a. Umpqua Bank

Financial banking services.

The concept was aimed at a new unique bank, with a special attitude to the client.

The solution was to exclude the formalities inherent in the banking sector. To make a shop out of the bank. Music is played in the premises of Umpqua Bank, coffee is drunk at the tables, and in the centre of the table, as at the market sale, there are various items scattered - from t-shirts to cups. The range of banking products includes: packaged in beautiful designer boxes describing tariff plans, credit cards, or mortgage programs.

Ordinary banks are cold, calm and boring. People cannot relax with them. To stand out, you need to make your stay at the bank pleasant.

As a result, they were able to create a new platform. Umpqua Bank has created a new kind of space for its customers, the third place between work and home, where you can spend time. Customers buy banking products as ordinary merchandise; they are interested in and consider offers. This reduces the pressure on the client to zero. And many people spend their free time in such shops, gather at them with friends.

German Airline Smintair

Air transportation of passengers.

Entering new markets to bring business to a global level

A bold decision to legalize smoking aboard planes. Specialize in the transportation of premium customers.

As a result, the smoking airline successfully engaged in the transportation of rich customers who prefer to be served by those who take into account their habits. Long-distance flights are especially popular. The demand for tickets is twice as high as the offer.

A Restaurant In Japan

They sell public catering. Prices are higher than average.

The concept required the creation of an institution where a large number of customers at the same time. To stand out from the ranks of competitors.

The mobility solution was the solution; the waiters had to serve customers by moving around the kilometre perimeter of the restaurant on roller skates. No one has ever had such a thing. Plus, this solution increases the speed of customer service in a vast area of the restaurant. As a result, the restaurant has gained world fame due to its uniqueness. At the same time, clients are served equally quickly regardless of the distance to the kitchen. The work of a waiter in this restaurant is considered to be very prestigious and profitable because you can get a tip for a change of an order of magnitude more than in conventional restaurants.

Toyota

Finding a solution to the problem of satisfying as many customers need as possible has led to an interesting idea.

It is an opportunity to come to the factory and order the manufacture of any model of Toyota, which has ever been produced. Even if they have already been taken out of production. For example, you like one of the Toyota models of 2001, and it's 2019. What should we do? We order the model of 2001 at the factory, and it is a new one, made in 2019, comes to you in the yard. It's a cool decision, you know.

This is an example of a strong customer focus. This is how customer loyalty is grown for centuries.

You have to realize that the system of your advantages must be in shape, which is the best way to answer the customer than you are better, your product or service?

Chapter 9. Marketing should be measured.

John Wanamaker - Creator of the price list. The price list has become the standard. Introduced a money-back guarantee, which is now standard business practice.

It gave its employees free medical care, education, recreational facilities, pensions, and profit-sharing.

He was the first retailer to place a half-page advertisement in a newspaper in 1874 and the first full-page advertisement in 1879. He created his ads, but later, he was the first in the world to hire a full-time copywriter, John Emory Powers. He was the one who said he knew that half of his marketing budget went into the pipe, but he didn't know which half.

Without knowing or understanding what marketing indicators need to be measured when conducting marketing activities, companies are throwing money away.

But the most critical indicators are not so much! And it is not difficult to analyze them at all; the main thing is to do it regularly. Therefore, I decided to highlight the most crucial marketing indicators for small and medium-sized businesses and show how to calculate them.

1. Important marketing indicators.

1. Distribution of marketing investments

Distribution of marketing investments is the basis of marketing planning. You can act like Vanamaker (as many entrepreneurs do, however) and say that I will make a month for marketing $500, and how they are used - I do not know. But then do not be surprised that some of them go to the wind.

Your marketing budget should be fully described in the marketing calendar, indicating what percentage of the budget is used in each marketing channel, as well as what goals you expect from each campaign.

In this way, you can identify and invest in more efficient channels of attraction.

2. Costs of attracting clients

The cost of attracting 1 client is one of the most important indicators. Knowing this figure, you can calculate the effectiveness of any client acquisition channel or marketing campaign. And based on the findings - to abandon inefficient channels and focus only on profitable and profitable ones.

The cost of attracting a client is calculated quite simply. You need to divide the cost of a marketing campaign (the number of marketing investments in a specific channel to attract customers) by the number of attracted customers.

3. Payback period of investments

To understand how quickly the investment in attracting a new client will pay off and whether it will pay off at all, it is essential to know a few additional indicators.

- Average sales amount

This indicator can be found out quite by merely taking the sales statistics for the same period last year, or the previous month. The average sales amount is calculated by dividing the sales amount by the number of customers who made the purchase.

- % markup

- Number of purchases per year

After the reallocation of investments, next month, we need to analyze how much each of the critical indicators has changed. Only then will you be able to determine the most effective proportions of the marketing budget distribution for each channel.

In addition to these 3 indicators, there are also essential marketing indicators, which also need to be measured regularly. This is the conversion and lifetime value of the client.

4. Conversion

The conversion shows what percentage of potential customers who responded to the advertisement made a purchase. The higher the conversion rate, the better the sales and marketing system in your company works. And the higher the profit. I wrote about it in content - marketing.

5. Lifetime value of the customer

Life long value of the client is an indicator of what profit the client will bring to your company for the whole period of cooperation. The author of the book Carl Sewell told about the lifetime value of the client

"I sell cars. In order not to complicate the calculations, we will consider that the average price of the car is $ 25,000. As a rule, the average client buys 10 cars from us during his life. That is $250,000. In addition, customers spend about a third of the price of servicing the machine. It gives about 82 500 $, and in total - 332 500. This amount can be earned by turning a customer of one machine into a customer for life.

Of course, this is a rough example. After all, it is necessary to consider the cost of attraction of the client, and also expenses for programs of the seduction of the client. But most importantly, this indicator makes you love your customers as soon as you know how much money they can bring to your company.

As Peter Ferdinand Drucker used to say: "What is not measured is not controlled. The same goes for marketing: if you don't measure the essential marketing indicators, you risk wasting money.

If you are a small or medium-sized business, you don't need an entire analytical department to measure key marketing indicators. There are very few of them so that you can analyze them yourself, or you can have them analyzed by your marketer.

Do your research every month. Find more efficient channels to attract and invest in your clients. Refuse from unfavourable channels of attracting clients.

Make your marketing predictable, controlled and effective!

Chapter 10. Marketing research? I'll think about it.

It's not always worth trusting marketing research. They are necessary, but their results should not obscure common sense.

Save yourself from making mistakes or why you shouldn't trust marketing research

You have to understand me right. I'm not an opponent of marketing research. Research is essential, but it has to be done professionally with an understanding of the purpose of the research.

Marketing research does not always provide reliable data.

Want to make sure? These are the stories of famous brands that market research has put an end to:

Sony Walkman

When the Sony Walkman portable player came on the market in 1979, it was a real revolution. Until then, nobody even thought that a person would be able to carry their favourite music everywhere.

Marketing research has shown that people "don't want to take a tape recorder everywhere. Anyway, Sony did not pay attention to this fact. And correctly done.

Player Sony Walkman not only brought world fame to the Japanese corporation but also created a new category of goods - portable music players. Its sales were kept at a high level for several decades. The company's problems came at the beginning of the XXI century when the Japanese insistently ignored mp-3 players and the transition to digital format. That's what they paid for. Today the world leader in the market of portable players is Apple with its iPod players.

Xerox

Today, photocopiers are an integral part of our lives. These names have become commonplace, representing not only the product of one particular company but also the whole category of products. However, at the end of the 40's the research conducted by Haloid Company (that's what Xerox was called before) showed that such a copying device is not needed by society. It is too expensive and uncomfortable.

It's a good thing that the company's management at that time had some smart people sitting around, and they didn't go for the research. As a result, in 1949, the first Xerox appeared on the market. And the commercial success of this product was so great that the company was later even renamed. In the 80s, Xerox became one of the most innovative companies in the United States. It is to it that the world owes not only copiers but also such concepts as a graphical window user interface and a computer mouse

Starbucks

Howard Schultz is a courageous guy. When he first started his business, most of the researchers unanimously said, "Show me a man who's willing to pay me $3 a cup of coffee. Howard Schultz showed millions of Americans. And then to the people of other countries.

Starbucks does not sell the best coffee. It cannot be compared to the best coffee houses in Italy. But, undoubtedly, the success of the company is explained by the atmosphere, which is carried by every cafe. Schultz once said he wanted Starbucks to be the third place between home and work for people.

And he has managed to realize his dreams thanks to the amazing atmosphere, but also because of the good quality of his coffee, which is not the best but is one of the best in the world.

Bell

At the end of the 19th century, Alexander Graham Bell and the partners were going to sell the Western Union company a patent for their new invention - the phone. This event went down in business history as the biggest mistake.

At the time, Western Union was a leader in the telegraph market. Naturally, progress did not stand still, and they needed to strengthen their position somehow. This may seem logical, but the company did not think so. When Bell and their comrades presented their invention at the WU, they were very disappointed. WU research has shown that a device like a phone has no future. Why is it necessary if there is a telegraph? And who would ever think of talking to someone on the phone? That's how Western Union rejected a company that would give birth to a murderer of a telegraph that almost destroyed the entire business of the company.

However, legend has it that WU did not conduct any research. The company just didn't like the idea of the phone. Perhaps so. Now they are engaged in money transfer and only partly remind the world of their former glory.

iPod

Apple's famous iPod, too, should not have been born if the company had trusted the results of market research. And they said that society did not need a hard drive player. People don't need to carry so many songs with them. Research has shown, but Steve Jobs thought differently. And once again, he was right because of his vision.

Today, the iPod is the most popular mp3 player, occupying in the world about 60% of the market. That's not to mention the fact that Apple has a quite popular accompanying product - the online music store iTunes Store.

These examples once again prove that research should only be an informative source, not a critical factor in decision-making. Only testing a product can show whether it will be in demand or has no future!

Chapter 11. Marketing - Budget.

There is no marketing without a budget! How much does a minute of your time cost? And now, calculate how many minutes you have already read the book? Multiply the number of minutes spent by their value and get a marketing investment budget! The secret of marketing is this: the more you invest in efficient marketing channels, the more you make a profit!

There are 2 suitable moments for marketing planning: yesterday and now.

Naturally, tomorrow we will not be able to return it, but we can easily use it for planning today. Many companies postpone planning to the end of the year. Many are waiting for the start of the new year to start planning. This is their crucial mistake. Marketing planning should always be done. There will be no better time than now for this.

1. Check - campaign planning sheet marketing.

That's why there's one mission waiting for you right now. Right now, answer 15 questions that will help you plan your company's marketing.

1.What marketing activities were successful in the past year?

Indicate only those events, the effect of which was obvious and was not questioned.

2.What marketing activities of the last year had partial success?

In this column, you can indicate the actions and events that were not included in answer to the first question.

3.What marketing activities did not have the required effect, or did not have any effect at all?

Here should be the marketing failures of last year.

4.Are there any obvious reasons why some actions were successful, and others were not?

Even if you can give a quick answer to this question, be sure to go back to it later and think about what you and not your counterpart did wrong.

5.Define your current target niche markets.

6.Do the customers you worked with last year belong to the current niche target markets?

7.Identify the niche markets you plan to enter in the coming year by the following criteria

- Geography
- Target audience
- Customer revenue level

8.Determine your marketing benefits by the following criteria:

- Your positioning
- Your unique selling proposition
- Benefits of clients from cooperation with you
- Useful marketing, what kind of question do you address
- How do you motivate clients to take action

9.Which of these components need to be strengthened, improved and clarified?

10.What new will you bring to your marketing advantages next year?

11.What channels and means will you use to deliver your marketing message next year?

Take into account the effectiveness of the channels and tools used last year, as well as the specifics of the target markets. Specify the desired amount. Later you will adjust it according to the advertising budget.

12.What are the channels and tools that have already been used? Will you use it again?

13.What new channels and means of marketing message delivery will you choose in the new year?

14.What is the frequency of use of each channel and methods, as well as the frequency of repetition of advertising campaigns?

15.What is your advertising budget for the next year and month?

Now everything is ready!

Using the received answers, we can proceed to the construction.

2. "The system of the full cycle of attracting and retaining clients."

Keys to mass customer acquisition

Any business starts with a plan. A plan to attract new customers and maintain relationships with existing customers. The plan for the development of the company and the adjustment of business processes. Before starting any business, it is important to know what sales volume is necessary for the company to develop and bring the expected income to the owner. To do this, of course, you need to know how many potential customers you need to have your company. It is not so difficult to know this amount - we will consider a detailed mechanism of how to determine how many potential customers you really need.

Also, we need to clearly know who our customers are, what their desires and needs are. What problems our product can solve and how it will help our client. One of the main mistakes of the beginning companies or the companies bringing a new product service to the market is an attempt to be "everything for everyone." It was also my mistake because

I was engaged in the widest possible aspect of marketing.

Not knowing their customers, companies spend a lot of money on ineffective advertising. And clients all do not appear. You already know the consequences of this.

The next step is to develop a "unique selling proposition." If clients do not understand the benefits of your offer and its differences from the competitors' offers, they start looking for the cheapest solution. Often, their choice will not be in your favour.

After these steps, companies face the following dilemma: how to reach their customers?

It doesn't matter to the customer "that your company has been in the market for 11 years" or "that you are pleased to offer cooperation. It is important to the client how you solve their problem or how you help them. But for the client to know this, they need to read your proposal first. It should catch the buyer and make him want to buy from you immediately.

Once the selling bid is written, the company should plan a marketing campaign. You don't have millions to risk and use expensive television advertising, do you? Or buy out your advertising blocks in the media. There are methods to advertise your products free of charge with the help of the media. You'll read this insider story a little later.

You have to choose the least expensive channels to attract customers and test the effectiveness of each of them. The most important thing is to use all channels and measure how much it costs you to draw a client through this channel and how many clients you receive through it. Then your advertising will be the most effective.

The final task before the company will be to obtain contacts from potential customers. Many customers will not buy your products at once. But in the future such a need they may have. Therefore, you always need to keep in touch with your customers. Moreover, your customers can give you valuable advice on how to improve and develop your business. And also bring new and new customers to you and recommend you to your friends.

How do we form a system?

3. We form the "client base plan."

There are undoubtedly those who underestimate and overlook this stage. Although it is, the beginning of all beginnings.

Before launching a new product, companies need to know how many promising customers it needs to develop. It is this figure that is the main reference point for the effective planning of marketing campaigns. Calculating it is not as difficult as you imagine. First of all, you need to predict your conversion rate. This is the number of customers that will buy your product.

For example, at the initial stage of the new product launch, you can predict that only 5 people out of 100 (or every twentieth customer) will buy your product. This means that your conversion is 5%. Next, you forecast the average purchase amount - the amount of money that the customer leaves with you for one purchase. For example, this amount is $5. The next step is to make an annual sales plan. You must set yourself the goals you want to achieve.

The goals should provide you with the expected profit and give you the opportunity to invest in the development of your business. If your annual sales plan is $12,000, then your monthly plan will be $1,000. Now we know your planned indicators:

- Conversion - 5%

- Your monthly sales plan is $1,000

- The average check is $5.

What do these numbers give us?

1) We can calculate how many transactions we need to make per month. In our case, it is 200 transactions (monthly sales plan/average check).

2) We can easily predict how many prospective clients we need per month. In our case, it is 1000 potential clients (number of transactions and * conversion rate).

It means that we need to attract 33 prospective clients per day (assuming that the number of days in a month is 30, you can also count on 21 working days), and this figure will be from 8300 to 12000 prospective clients per year. This is how we set the benchmark.

This is a universal approach. If the conversion is higher or the average amount of the check is different, the number of prospective customers needed can be significantly reduced.

4. Where can I get clients? Channels of attraction.

In order to systematically attract new customers, you need to know what channels work effectively. With a limited budget, you need to choose inexpensive channels to attract. Let's consider them:

E-mail

If you already have contacts with potential customers, you can send them commercial offers.

Your site

On the site, you can offer to register to a potential client or subscribe to the newsletter in exchange for any gift. This can be a discount, certificate, free product

PR You can write articles in editions that are read by your target audience. Give a lot of advice and link it to your product or service. For example, if you sell furniture, you can write an article entitled "5 criteria for choosing good furniture". Of course, your furniture must meet all 5 criteria.

Cold calls

Cold calls are a very effective way of doing things. If your company has great salespeople, the conversion of calls will be very high. Be sure to use cold calls when attracting new customers.

Affiliate programs

A lot of clients can be attracted through partners. To do this, you will need to negotiate with non-competing companies working with the same target audience. Mutual PR and recommendations, as well as deductions for sales to these customers, are the points of interaction for you.

Conducting free seminars and webinars

You can gather your target audience and hold free seminars for them. You can solve some small problem with potential clients. This way, customers will have more confidence in you and your products.

As in the articles, you can give useful advice related to your products. The big advantage of such seminars is that you will be able to sell your products on the spot and get new customers.

Business cards

You can make your business cards sell. On the backside of your business card, put a piece of brief information about your products and promise the business card bearer a gift or additional discount. Many potential customers will definitely take advantage of this opportunity.

Recommendations

Ask your friends if they know anybody who might benefit from your products? Ask your friends to recommend you. This is often a way to attract a lot of new customers. Also, with the help of recommendations, you can establish new affiliate programs and give your friends an additional opportunity to earn money. All advertising campaigns, even if they are free, need to be carefully planned. You should know exactly which channels work effectively and which do not. Let's talk about it now for the last time.

1. Selling Bidding Proposal. How to avoid mistakes?

A quotation is an advertisement text and an official document. It is the place where every businessman without exception is trapped. Often the commercial offer becomes the weakest link of the company. Even if the unique trading offer is clearly defined and the target audience is identified. The reason for the typical mistakes in the preparation of commercial proposals:

1. Unattractive headline. Remember why the yellow press is bought? Because of the headlines! The title should make you want to read the sentence to the end, not to push away the client. For example; "commercial proposal" is a bad title.

2. A unique selling proposition is not specified. The client does not understand how this offer differs from the rest Overloaded terms. If the client does not understand the complex terms used in the sentence, he stops reading it.

3. Blanket text. When a sentence is written in solid text, it is very hard to read. Therefore, it is essential to remember that the majority of customers will not read until the end of the commercial offer.

4. There is no time limit. If there is no time limit on the duration of the commercial offer, the client usually takes a break to think about it. Often this thinking is delayed for eternity. Show your determination and specificity, always specify the dates.

5. No contact information. If the client is interested in the offer but does not find any contacts, they are unlikely to contact the company. Such an approach can occur if it is a developed activity in the form of a quest. But it is unlikely that all your new customers like quests.

6. Inaction. There is no clear call to action, what exactly should a potential client do after reading the commercial offer. Buy, contact, call, save.

7. Long offers. Long sentences severely impair the readability of the text. This is a private reason not to read through the whole sentence

8. Banal and meaningless phrases. "We are glad to offer you cooperation" and "Our company has been in the market for 10 years" or "We are client-oriented" and "Seasonal discount" lead to the fact that the commercial offer is in the garbage can, and the e-mail address is marked as spam.

I think this is a good field for a new round in your new commercial offer

2. Is my marketing effective? Marketing activity indicators.

Increased sales with the same budget.

Let's look at the situation. You use marketing. Your strategy includes three different activities. In the end, you get a plus. But if we measure them separately, we can reduce the costs of inefficient marketing and increase them into effective marketing.

Important indicators for measuring your marketing

1. Customer Acquisition Cost (CAC)

This is the total cost of marketing and sales - the total cost of attracting 1 client. To calculate the index, it is necessary to add up all the expenses for advertising, salaries, commissions, and bonuses. Overhead costs for a certain period and divide by the number of new clients for the same period. It can be a month, a quarter, or a year. For example, if you spent $100,000 on sales and marketing in a month and attracted 10 new clients, then your CAC is $10,000.

2. Marketing part of the customer acquisition cost (M%-CAC)

From the total cost of attracting the client, "CAC" allocate a part of the total cost, which falls on the marketing. This indicator can be called M%-CAC - it reflects what share of CAC is the marketing cost of customer attraction. It is useful to observe this indicator in dynamics - any change signals that something has changed in your strategy or your efficiency.

For example, an increase in M%-CAC can mean

-You spend too much on marketing

-Sales costs are lower because they receive less funding

-You are trying to increase your sales productivity through additional investment in marketing, and better and more active marketing leads to sales

For companies with long and complicated sales cycles, M%-CAC can be only 10-20%. For companies that have low cost and simple sales cycle, including automated, this figure can be 60-90%.

3. Customer Life Cycle Assessment Ratio "Life Time Value" to CAC (LTV: CAC)

Companies that have a constant flow of income from their customers through repeat sales need to assess revenues from existing customers and compare them with the cost of attracting new ones. For this purpose, the customer's life cycle assessment indicator "LTV - lifetime value" is used. The indicator allows estimating the net income which the company can receive from the buyer during all its life cycle.

In order to calculate LTV, you must determine the marginal profit that the customer brings to you for a certain period "per year" and divide it by the estimated percentage of outflow of "refusal to buy" for the period for this type of customers.

When you know the LTV and CAC figures, you can calculate their ratio. A higher ratio means that your sales and marketing have a relatively high ROI. The higher the ROI, the more clients you attract and retain, the more profit you make and the equal cost of attracting one.

In growing companies, most investors and board members will want to see this ratio greater than 3:1. More, however, does not mean better. When this ratio is too high, it makes sense to spend more on sales and marketing to stimulate overall revenue growth, because by holding back your marketing costs, you will only make life easier for competitors.

4. Payback time for CAC

This is the number of months it takes to recoup the cost of attracting new customers. It's simple - take the CAC index, divide by the average margin received from transactions with new clients per month, and get the number of months during which we will recoup the CAC.

In industries where clients pay once in advance, this index is less relevant, because the prepayment must be higher than CAC; otherwise, you lose money on each client.

On the other hand, in industries where customers pay monthly or annual fees, it is usually required that the payback period is less than 12 months, so you will reach the payback point within a year and then start earning a net profit.

5. Marketing contribution to customer engagement (in %)

To calculate it, you need to take the total number of clients you have attracted in the reporting period and see what percentage of them are attracted by marketing. This is much easier to do when you have a marketing analytics system, but you can do it manually - just take longer to do it. This metric clearly reflects the role of marketing in attracting clients, and, very often, the contribution of marketing is higher than the share of attracted clients at the expense of sales. This indicator varies from company to company. For example, in companies with a dedicated sales department working on cold calls, it can be quite low 20-30%, and, conversely, for companies with an automated sales process, it can be 65-95%.

Note: You can also calculate this indicator as a percentage of revenue received rather than attracted customers, depending on how you prefer to look at your business.

6. Marketing impact on customers

The indicator is very similar to the previous one, but it takes into account all clients covered by marketing activities, not just those attracted at their expense. For example, if a customer was attracted by the sales department but had previously participated in one of the marketing activities (e.g., received advertising), he or she is also counted in this indicator because he or she was influenced by marketing activities. Obviously, the percentage of this indicator is higher than the previous one and averages from 50 to 99%.

With the help of these indicators, you will be able to understand how effectively the marketing campaign has passed.

3. Tips that bring in money.

1. The secret to the power of the postscript

The most readable place is not a title. Numerous studies have shown that the first part of any letter that is read to the end is a postscript. In second place is the title. Very few copywriters use this technique

P.S. Postscript helps to significantly improve the advertising text and increase the percentage of responses to it.

P.S. Do you use P.S. in your advertising materials?

2. Record deadlines

Offer recipients something of value that they can get for free, provided that they respond immediately, and that it is unattainable in any other way. The offer must match what you are selling. For example, if you were a tax accountant trying to attract new customers for the next year, you could send a mailing list in January of the coming year that would offer the first 101 new customers a free leather folder to keep their tax records for the past year.

It would have to be indicated that this offer is valid until March 10. Potential customers who cannot afford to delay would act immediately.

3. Save holiday cards

Experience has shown that a classic letter in an envelope is much more likely to cause a response from recipients. Most consumers receive important messages in their letters, which is very personal. Even the action of printing the envelope and unfolding the letter is intriguing.

An example of a successful implementation. The company has created a two-page letter for a firm that has sold a $1,000 annual subscription to advertisers and advertising agencies. The client did quite well with the postcard campaign.

The effectiveness was about 0.85% of paid applications

Further, the letter for advertising agencies in which it was spoken has been created: "If you send me by e-mail a code from 4 letters specified above I shall send you a secret which will help you to organize new business, in the not occupied niche about which you even would not think at all. Each recipient had his or her own personal code, which is written in the letter only.

The level of paid orders, in response to the campaign, increased to 12%.

4. Highlight the benefits of your product, not just its features

Let's say you're selling a teapot with a spout that keeps the liquid from leaking past the dishes. Instead of just mentioning the special design of the spout, you need to pay attention to the problems that can be avoided thanks to it: burnt hands, spoiled things, and so on. How do you understand what characteristics of your product are most valuable for consumers? Ask them. For example, if you sell a kettle that is sealed and does not leak, you can talk to the tea buyers at the local supermarket to find out what kettles they use and how these kettles can be improved.

5. Outperform your competitors

If your business is a competing dry-cleaner, dry-cleaner "ABC Cleaners", located on the same street, offers a discount of 15% for new customers, then extend your regular customers a 20% discount as an incentive to maintain loyalty to you.

6. Use photos of real people

When we use photos of real customers or employees, not models, in the mailing lists, the response to the campaign increases. You can apply this technique to your strategy.

7. Use the right databases

Companies selling databases will offer you to buy a variety of types of databases. You will need to request those whose contact persons gave the highest percentage of responses to offers and products that are identical to yours.

8. Use a personal approach

If your letter and envelope look as if they have been in the person's hands at some stage of preparation and sending, there is a higher chance that the client will open it. Sign your letter in blue ink. Highlight a paragraph with a different colour or mark the margins with a different colour. Try putting a real stamp on the envelope. The more non-standard stamps they are, the better. In this e-mailed world, a human touch can have a fantastic impact. While most companies continue to fill up their potential customers with countless offers and contextual advertising, you can start growing your customers tomorrow.

Manifesto.

The stage of development of the process in which you participate has its own period. This period is 6 months. Every 6 months, draw a line for yourself. Assess where you are, what is your current status? Look at the tasks you have accomplished, the tasks you have accomplished, or the tasks you have not achieved. Everything will come down to the conclusion that your life is work, priorities, stress, deadline. Your life is a taste of victory, triumph, and self-satisfaction. Search for new ways and new solutions. Add creativity and enjoy it! You have to understand that most people can't do what you can! I have always preferred a sprint marathon. In the initial stage, many people light up, and can even burn brighter than you, be faster and more active. Later, they lose the inner fire, the fire in their eyes. They want to burn and are looking for those who continue to carry fire for other people. There are no drawbacks - these are your growth areas. The best time now. Rhythm, the universal thing that with its vibrations and pace, overcomes everything in its path! Transform yourself!

Inspiration.

Branding, Marketing, Sales. My formation as a manager has taken place in national and transnational campaigns. I was an employee. I accepted the conditions of the game, tried to improve and refine them. After reading the works of professor Philip Kotler, I found a lot of interesting and field to study. All my passion and knowledge were combined into projects. I was looking for a book that could solve several questions at once. A general understanding of the whole marketing picture, which can be used in the work of several focus groups. I was looking for a unified formula to measure marketing, efficiency, loyalty, sales. I am giving you this experience, filled with failures and successes. This book, a guide who will be relevant to you always. It is a book for the best, and the best must always be improved! The world has accelerated, and the knowledge required transformation, refinement, improvement. I was inspired by you and felt the invisible connection that passes between the continents. At its root, it is evolution. It is the development that moved our planet, our ancestors. You, like me, are looking for new keys to a new gate. So let us do it together! Keep carrying the torch for new people!

www.ingramcontent.com/pod-product-compliance
Lightning Source LLC
Chambersburg PA
CBHW021410210526
45463CB00001B/303